EXTREME
Spot the Difference

WONDERS OF
THE WORLD

40 High-Resolution
Photo Puzzles

THUNDER BAY
P·R·E·S·S
San Diego, California

Thunder Bay Press

An imprint of the Baker & Taylor Publishing Group
10350 Barnes Canyon Road, San Diego, CA 92121
www.thunderbaybooks.com

Copyright © Carlton Books Ltd, 2014

All notations of errors or omissions should
be addressed to Thunder Bay Press, Editorial
Department, at the above address. All other
correspondence (author inquiries, permissions)
concerning the content of this book should be
addressed to Carlton Books Limited, 20 Mortimer
Street, London W1T 3JW.
info@carltonbooks.co.uk

ISBN-13: 978-1-62686-249-4
ISBN-10: 1-62686-249-4

Printed in China.
1 2 3 4 5   18 17 16 15 14

CONTENTS

Introduction	08
How to Play	12

THE PUZZLES 14

Puzzle 01	Taj Mahal	16
Puzzle 02	Rio Carnival	20
Puzzle 03	Las Vegas	24
Puzzle 04	Taktsang Monastery	28
Puzzle 05	Marrakech	32
Puzzle 06	Athens	36

Puzzle 07	Bora Bora	40
Puzzle 08	India	44
Puzzle 09	Mexico City	48
Puzzle 10	Colosseum	52
Puzzle 11	Copacabana	56
Puzzle 12	Delhi	60
Puzzle 13	Palace of Versailles	64
Puzzle 14	Potala Palace	68
Puzzle 15	Dubai	72
Puzzle 16	St. Basil's Cathedral	76
Puzzle 17	Stockholm	80
Puzzle 18	Venice	84
Puzzle 19	Fort Lauderdale	88
Puzzle 20	Old Jerusalam	92
Puzzle 21	Étretat	96
Puzzle 22	Hagia Sophia	100
Puzzle 23	Ho Chi Minh City	104
Puzzle 24	United States Capitol	108

Puzzle 25 Santorini   112

Puzzle 26 River Thames   116

Puzzle 27 Persepolis   120

Puzzle 28 Peru   124

Puzzle 29 Petra   128

Puzzle 30 Central Park   132

Puzzle 31 Krakow   136

Puzzle 32 Cinque Terre   140

Puzzle 33 Xijiang Miao   144

Puzzle 34 St. Peter's Square   148

Puzzle 35 Thanksgiving Day Parade   152

Puzzle 36 Dragon Boat Race   156

Puzzle 37 Salamanca   160

Puzzle 38 Himalayas   164

Puzzle 39 Battle of the Oranges   168

Puzzle 40 Niagara Falls   172

Photo Credits   176

INTRODUCTION

Our planet is full of wonders. Natural, ancient, modern, or simple, popular tourist hotspots, no matter what you call them, are all indeed wonder-full.

Extreme Spot the Difference: Wonders of the World is action-packed with the planet's most attractive, far-flung locations; an exotic feast for the eyes and brain. For anyone who has ever wanted to get up close and personal with the great pyramids of Giza, or the Hagia Sophia, or the belly-dancers of the Rio Carnival—this is your chance. And, what's more, you don't need to find your passport, book an airline ticket, or even pack a suitcase. These wonders will appear right before your eyes!

Transporting you across the globe to the most captivating locales deemed as official "wonders" by all those lucky enough to have traveled there, this book is the world's best travel guide—with a difference. From the Taktsang Monastery to the tranquil lagoons of Bora Bora, stopping off en route in Salamanca before making a splashdown in the iconic falls of Niagara, this puzzle book will leave you in awe of the world and, we hope, scratching your head in bemused wonder at what you see... and what you don't!

Throughout human history, not only has mankind sought to adventure the globe, we have also devised inventive ways of expanding and challenging our minds. Mankind's love of puzzles, riddles, and brainteasers dates back thousands of years and as we have evolved, so, too, have the puzzles. The book you now hold in your hands represents the pinnacle of modern puzzle challenges using high-resolution photography and advanced image manipulation technology to cover the world's greatest wonders in spectacular detail.

This colorful guide will transport you all over the globe, from the cloud-bursting skyscrapers of Dubai, to the markets of Marrakech, to the annual Thanksgiving Day Parade in New York City. All you have to do is pick up your pen, turn the page, and you're ready to travel.

Tougher, more engaging, and more visually extraordinary than any other puzzle book you've seen before, this impressive collection of photographs boasts some tough mental tests. Challenge your visual powers with forty high resolution spot-the-difference scenes, each with fifty imaginative and often surprising changes for you to find.

As predominantly visual creatures, we make sense of our world through our eyes. It's the main reason why people have come to love spot-the-difference puzzles so much. They naturally complement the way our brains work; the visual stimulus offers our brains—via our eyes—a problem it can't wait to solve. Like athletes' muscles, our brains can lose their stamina and fitness if they are not tried and tested often.

On the pages of this book you will find an amazing range of gorgeous, finely detailed images to delight the eye, and something better: a chance for the brain to really exercise its visual comparison circuitry.

The wonders explored in the following pages combine two of humankind's favorite passions: puzzles and traveling, all in one. However, *Extreme Spot the Difference: Wonders of the World* is much more than just an ordinary spot the difference collection. The challenges before you encourage you to interact with what you see,

flex and test your brain and eye muscles, and have some extreme fun!

With all that in mind, accept the challenge this unique and fascinating book has to offer. You'll be rewarded not only with a massive sense of achievement at completing the tasks, your brain will also transform into a leaner, quick-thinking super-computer—a puzzle-solving machine. In the process you may even ignite a passion for puzzles that you'll take with you in all areas of your life.

So, find a comfortable chair and let's go on an adventure that encompasses the world's most cherished wonders, and discover what amazing sights they have to offer. Where will you go first? The challenge is set... off you go!

HOW TO PLAY

There are forty puzzles in *Extreme Spot the Difference: Wonders of the World*. Each has their own complex and unique aesthetic just like the location itself. There are fifty differences per wonder to find. Best to get comfy. The puzzle changes are an entertaining mix of the obvious (once you have seen them), and the ingenious. As well as being a supreme test of your observation skills, we are confident that you will find this book lots of fun, and it will keep you occupied for hours!

With 2,000 extreme differences to find, you are going to have your work cut out as you attempt to identify all of the changes, so here are a few handy hints and tips to help you on your way.

Before you begin, have a pen and some paper on hand so you can write down the coordinates of the differences as you find them. The original unaltered photograph is shown on the left page, followed by the changed version on the right. Note the pink coordinate on your paper, and then the blue coordinate as this is how you will find them listed on the answer key. The answer key appears immediately after each puzzle.

To help with your hunt, we've included a unique aid for you—the Spotter's Grid. Place it over the picture to isolate a small section, then easily compare with its near twin on the other page. Circling the differences on the Spotter's Grid will also allow you to share the puzzles with others without giving away all the answers. Wipe it clean after each puzzle to use it again and again. Armed with your Spotter's Grid and your powers of observation, all that's left to say is best of luck and happy hunting!

124 125

PUZZLE 28: Peru

126

PUZZLE 28

Peru

The Republic of Peru is a country in the west of South America, bordering Bolivia, Brazil, Chile, Colombia, Ecuador, and the Pacific Ocean. While 60 percent of Peru may be covered in Amazon rainforests, the country also boasts some very beautiful coastal areas.

01-02	14-15	Changed: height of building	15-18	18	Changed: height of wall
01-02	25-25	Added: tree	16-17	30	Added: shadow
01-02	29-31	Added: tree	18-19	22-23	Removed: shadow
01-04	33-35	Added: tree	19-20	10-13	Changed: height of building
03-09	03-06	Added: seagull	19	20	Removed: figure
02-03	20	Removed: vehicle	20	17-18	Changed: sculpture, red to purple
03-03	28	Removed: person	20-22	19-21	Changed: greenery to dirt
03-04	26	Removed: wrapped paraglider	22		Added: mud
04-08	09-10	Removed: building	22	14-15	Changed: height of sculpture
04-08	18	Removed: path	22-23	23-24	Added: seagull
04-05	19	Added: vehicle	23-08	03-10	Added: paraglider
04	29	Changed: shirts, red to blue	23	15	Removed: small building
05-06	33-34	Removed: waste container	24	21-22	Removed: vehicle
06-07	20-22	Added: tree	25-27	14-15	Changed: extended beach
06-07	31-32	Added: path section	25		Removed: vehicle
07	14-15	Removed: top of tree	25-26	16-17	Added: tree
07-08	32-33	Removed: path section	27	25	Added: bushes
08-11	28-29	Changed: size of shadow	27-28	33-34	Added: seagull
09-10	10-11	Removed: top of building	28-30	11-13	Added: paraglider
09-11	24-26	Changed: parachute, orange to blue	28-30	19-21	Added: paraglider
09-10	33-33	Changed: length of block	28	19-20	Removed: shadow
11-12	07-09	Changed: height of building	28-29	22-23	Removed: vehicle
11-14	32-33	Added: greenery	25	25	Removed: vehicle
12	25-29	Removed: shadow	28	30	Added: vehicle
14-16	24-25	Changed: graphic, blue to red	29-30	15-16	Removed: paraglider

127

THE PUZZLES

PUZZLE 01

Taj Mahal

The Taj Mahal is a white marble mausoleum located in Agra, India. It was constructed in 1648 on the orders of the Mughal emperor Shah Jahan to commemorate his beloved wife Mumtaz Mahal.

01–03	20–21	Added: rim	14–15	05–07	Changed: spire bent
01–05	30–35	Added: tiger	15–16	14–16	Added: tower
02–05	02–04	Added: parakeet	15–16	26	Removed: windows
03	25	Removed: window	16–18	22–23	Added: arch window
03–04	25–27	Changed: height of tree	16–17	28–29	Added: panel
04	15–17	Changed: height of tower	16–19	29	Changed: height of fence
04–05	29–33	Changed: tree	16–19	33–35	Added: tiger in water
05–06	22–23	Changed: archway	18	14–16	Added: tower
06	17–18	Removed: tower	19–20	26	Changed: size of panel
07–11	16	Changed: height of base	19–22	32–33	Removed: tree reflections
07–10	35	Added: water lilies	20–23	16	Changed: height of base
08–09	20–21	Added: arch window	21–23	35	Added: water lilies
08–09	28–31	Added: tree	22	13	Changed: height of spire
09	13–14	Removed: spire	22	17–18	Removed: inside arch
09	17–18	Removed: inside arch	22	22–23	Removed: doorway
09	22–23	Removed: doorway	22	25–26	Changed: height of window
09	25–26	Changed: height of window	22–23	29–31	Added: tree
10–11	27–29	Added: arch	25	17–18	Removed: tower
11–19	18	Changed: stone section	25–26	20–21	Changed: height of arch
11–12	26	Changed: size of panel	25–26	26–27	Changed: archway
11–13	34–35	Changed: reflection	27	15–17	Changed: height of tower
12–14	29	Changed: height of fence	28–29	17–19	Removed: top of tower
13–14	12–13	Removed: bricks	28–30	23–24	Added: rim
13	14–16	Added: tower	28	32–33	Removed: hole
13–14	22–23	Added: arch window	29–30	27–32	Added: tree

PUZZLE 02

Rio Carnival

Possibly the largest and most famous annual carnival in the world, this lavish festival begins on the Friday before Lent in Rio de Janeiro, Brazil. The floats and parades are created by local samba schools.

01	17	Added: speaker
01–02	04–07	Added: windows
01–02	30–32	Added: head decoration
02–04	31–32	Removed: camera
03–05	34–35	Changed: shirt, blue to green
03–04	14–15	Added: speaker
04–05	32–33	Added: head decoration
05	30	Added: light
05–06	01–02	Added: spotlight
05–07	02–03	Removed: tree branch
06–09	10–11	Added: gold edging
07	26–27	Removed: head
07–10	28–35	Added: bear
08	06	Removed: orb
08–09	14–17	Changed: fan section, red to yellow
08–10	20–21	Changed: top of vase, red to green
08–12	08–10	Changed: fan, red to green
10–11	06–07	Changed: triangle, yellow to blue
11–12	04	Removed: window
12–13	01–02	Changed: length of whiteboard
12–13	17–18	Removed: wrist decoration
13–14	24	Removed: arm
14–15	02–03	Added: decoration
14–15	12–13	Changed: ball, gray to red
14–16	29–31	Removed: head

15–16	03–05	Removed: white line
15–17	09–11	Changed: triangle, red to green
16	01–02	Removed: green line
16–17	05–06	Changed: length of feather
16–17	13	Removed: white stripe
16–20	20–26	Added: totem pole
17–18	02–03	Removed: circular design
17–18	14–15	Changed: size of tambourine
18–19	14–15	Removed: shoulder decoration
20–21	01–02	Added: lights
20	16–17	Removed: arm band
21–22	05–06	Changed: decoration, pink to green
22–24	03–04	Removed: white panels
22–26	08–10	Changed: fan, red to purple
22–23	12–15	Changed: fan section, red to yellow
22–23	27–28	Changed: fabric, gray to green
22–24	30–33	Changed: width of wooden section
23–25	01–02	Added: eagle
24–25	25–26	Added: person
24–25	28–31	Removed: blue mesh
25–26	03–04	Removed: sign
25–26	14–17	Added: rosette
25–26	20–21	Added: vase
26–28	06–08	Changed: triangle, yellow to red
29–30	14–20	Changed: width of gold section

PUZZLE 03

Las Vegas

Established in 1905 in southern Nevada, Las Vegas has become one of the world's top tourist destinations. It is internationally famous for its gargantuan gambling establishments, glitzy nightlife, and nonstop entertainment.

01–02	31–32	Added: hedge
01–03	18–20	Added: dollar bill
01–05	01–08	Added: cloud
03–06	17–18	Changed: sign, pink to cyan
03–04	21–22	Removed: round sign
04	20–21	Removed: guitar tuner
04–05	28	Changed: sign, green to red
04–05	31	Changed: flowers, pink to blue
04–05	32	Removed: people
04–05	33–34	Changed: taxi top, green to red
05	20–21	Removed: lettering from guitar
06–10	02–04	Added: playing card
06–07	10–12	Added: building section
06–07	24–25	Changed: width of building
06–12	18–19	Added: roller coaster
08–09	30–31	Changed: vehicle, red to green
08–09	31–32	Removed: vehicle
08–10	35	Added: bush
10–12	15	Changed: building section
11–14	33–35	Added: bush
13–15	18–25	Changed: building, green to pink
13–15	29–30	Removed: vehicle
14–22	07–10	Added: playing card
14–15	13–15	Removed: top of building
15–16	25	Removed: window

15–17	30–31	Removed: vehicle
15–18	33–34	Removed: median strip
16–17	14	Removed: top of building
16–18	17–20	Removed: building section
18	24	Removed: roof section
18–21	27	Added: stonework
19–21	29	Removed: vehicle
19–21	32–34	Added: playing card
20–21	14–16	Changed: height of building
20–21	19–23	Removed: roller coaster section
22	26–27	Removed: window
22–24	22	Removed: roller coaster section
23–23	16–17	Changed: height of building
23–24	26	Removed: window
24–30	09–12	Added: cloud
24	30–31	Changed: trailer, green to red
24–30	31–35	Added: dollar
25	25–26	Added: columns
26–27	27–29	Added: elevator section
27–30	23–24	Removed: roller coaster section
28–30	30	Removed: building writing
29–30	25–26	Changed: roof, blue to red
28–30	28–29	Changed: length of bus
30	23	Added: building extension
30	29–30	Removed: vehicle

PUZZLE 04

Taktsang Monastery

Paro Taktsang (also known as "Tiger's Nest") is a Buddhist holy site and temple, built in 1692 and situated in the Paro Valley of the Himalayas. The legendary Guru Rinpoche is said to have been carried to the cave on the back of a flying tigress where he then meditated and emerged in eight incarnated forms.

02	20–21	Removed: blue flag
03–05	33–35	Changed: flag, blue to yellow
03–06	10–18	Added: waterfall
05–11	30–35	Added: red flag
07–09	28–29	Changed: flag, red to blue
08–10	01–11	Removed: white flags
09–11	29–30	Changed: cloth, red to blue
09–14	14–20	Added: line of flags
10–12	11–12	Added: rock painting
11	21–22	Added: pink shirt
12–16	05–11	Changed: rock pattern flipped
13	14	Added: window
14	14–15	Changed: enlarged bell
15	18–19	Removed: window
15–17	18–19	Added: length to roof
15–16	11–12	Changed: height of roof decoration
15–16	17	Added: roof
15–18	32–34	Changed: direction of flag
16	14	Changed: circle to square
16	21	Added: person
17	15–16	Removed: window
17–18	15–18	Added: steps
17–20	29–32	Removed: cracks on rock surface
18–19	19	Added: shed
19	24–26	Removed: red flag

19–20	12	Changed: size of window
19–20	11	Removed: top of window
19–21	09	Added: flags
19–20	16–17	Added: window
19–23	16	Changed: wall, red to blue
21	14	Removed: golden circle
21	21–22	Added: rock painting
21–22	14	Removed: window
21–24	13	Changed: roof, red to yellow
22–23	09	Added: roof decoration
22–23	15	Removed: wall
23–24	03	Added: seated person
23–25	29–32	Added: blue flag
24–25	22–23	Added: person
24–25	08–09	Removed: flags
24–25	11	Added: person
24–25	08	Added: chimney
25–30	01–07	Added: beam of sunlight
26	07–08	Changed: bigger roof decoration
26	10–11	Removed: window
27–29	22–23	Added: goat
27–29	29–31	Added: green flag
28–30	05–07	Added: mountain
29–30	13–15	Added: fire
30	07–10	Added: pylon

PUZZLE 05

Marrakech

Marrakech is one of Morocco's major metropolitan areas, and the greatest of its former Imperial cities. It is famous for its souks—open air market places.

01	11–14	Added: window
01–02	04–05	Removed: umbrella
01–03	26–28	Removed: cart wheel
01–04	22–24	Changed: carriage, green to red
01–07	32–34	Added: palm tree
03–04	31	Removed: writing on jacket
03–05	07–08	Removed: air conditioner
04	29–30	Changed: hat, blue to red
05	21–22	Changed: shirt, yellow to pink
06	19–20	Changed shirt, red to orange
06–07	29–30	Changed: shirt, green to orange
08	03–04	Removed: railing
08–09	26–30	Removed: person
09–10	18–21	Removed: pillar
09–10	31–32	Removed: shadow
10	25	Removed: red triangle
10–11	34–35	Removed: person's shadow
10–13	01–04	Removed: antenna
11–12	21–25	Changed: width of display
11–14	04–06	Changed: banner, red to green
12–13	08–09	Removed: lantern
12–15	14–15	Removed: writing on sign
13–14	24–25	Changed: shirt, red to blue
15–17	17–18	Removed: awning section
16–17	07–12	Added: window

17–18	01–02	Removed: person
17–19	29–30	Changed: coat, orange to green
18–19	25–28	Removed: person
18–22	11–14	Added: palm tree
19–21	08	Changed: width of green roof
20–21	17–18	Removed: lantern
20–25	01–02	Changed: roof, green to pink
21	04–06	Changed: height of window
22	19–20	Removed: lightbulb
22–23	25–26	Removed: yellow box
23	04–07	Removed: window
23–24	22	Added: stripe to column
23–24	34	Removed: logo from sweatshirt
23–25	27–28	Changed: box, blue to pink
23–27	16	Removed: sign wire
24–25	02–06	Changed: tiles, green to orange
25	18–20	Added: opening
25–26	22–23	Removed: sign
25–26	24–25	Removed: stripe from column
25–27	11–12	Removed: person
28–29	25	Removed: stripe from column
28–29	28	Changed: shirt, blue to pink
29–30	07	Added: light
29–30	19–20	Changed: shutter, red to green
29–30	34–35	Changed: leggings, blue to green

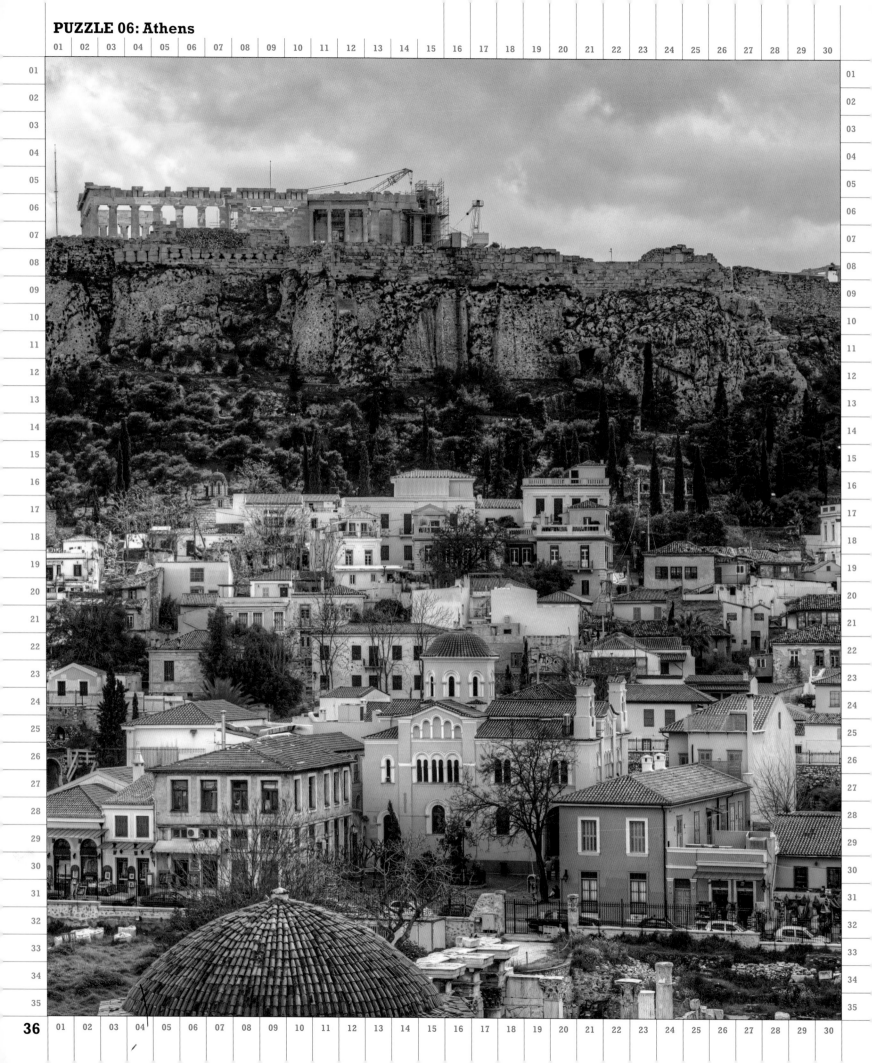

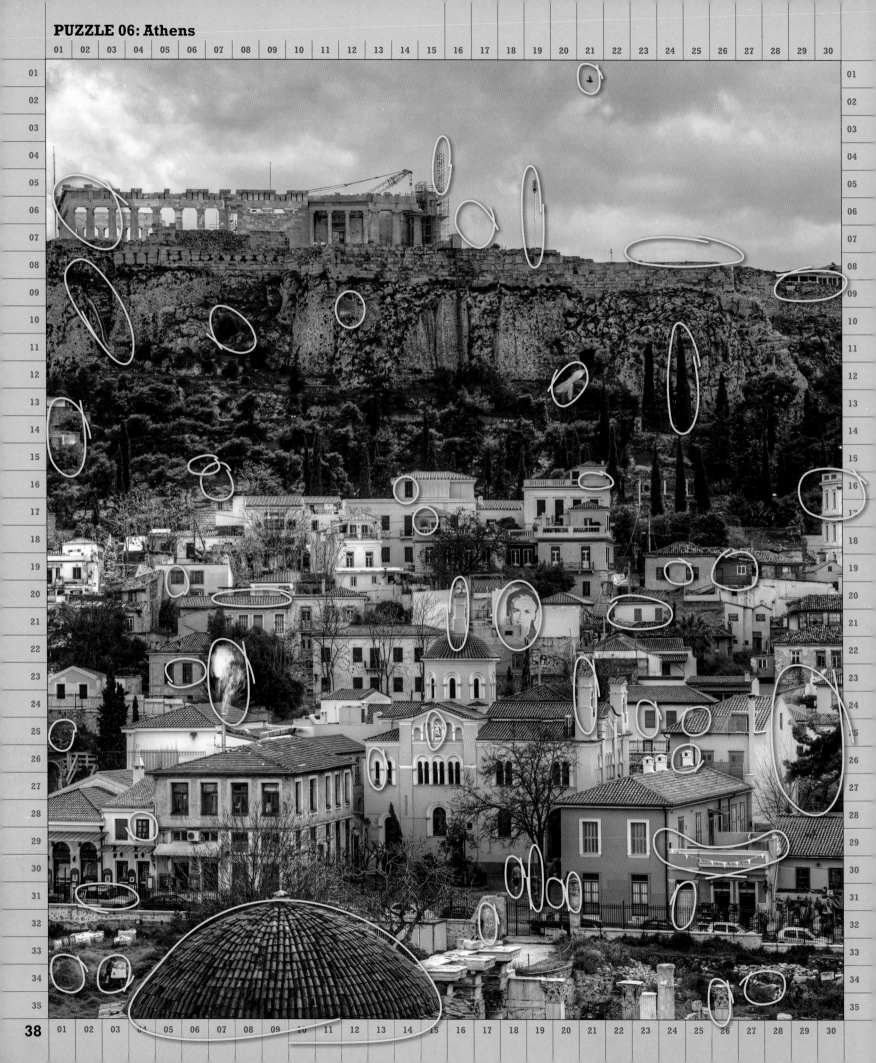

PUZZLE 06

Athens

Athens is the capital of Greece and one of the oldest cities in the world. It was home to many of the Classical Era's greatest philosophers and is known as the cradle of Western Civilization. Modern Athens is a cosmopolitan city and a member of the European Union.

01	25	Removed: arched entrance
01–02	13–15	Added: house
01–02	34	Added: haystack
01–03	05–07	Added: extra ruins
01–04	08–12	Added: walled pathway
02–03	31	Changed: car, brown to green
03	33–34	Added: picnic table
04	28–29	Changed: window
04–15	31–35	Changed: roof, brown to green
05–06	19–20	Added: window
06	23	Added: window
06–07	15	Added: cow
06–07	16	Removed: roof dome
07–08	22–24	Added: smoke
07–08	10–11	Added: cave
07–10	20	Changed: extended roof
12	09–10	Added: graffiti
13	26–27	Added: window
14	16	Added: window
15	17	Changed: bush, yellow to green
15	25	Added: statue
15	04–05	Added: extra scaffolding
16	20–21	Added: monument on rooftop
16–17	06–07	Removed: crane
17	32	Removed: utility box

18	30–31	Added: person
18–21	20–21	Added: wall graffiti
19	30–31	Changed: call box, yellow to red
19	05–07	Added: floodlight
20–21	12–13	Added: lava
20	31	Removed: person
20	30–31	Added: height to pillar
21	01	Added: bird
21	23–25	Added: roof extension
21	16	Removed: pillars
23	24–25	Changed: shutter, brown to green
23–26	07–08	Removed: wall
24	19	Removed: window
24–25	11–14	Added: tree
22–24	20–21	Changed: building, pink to yellow
24–25	26	Added: chimney
24–25	31–32	Changed: door, blue to yellow
24–27	29–30	Added: flags
25	24–25	Removed: roof screen
26	34–35	Added: pillar
26–27	19	Changed: house, orange to blue
27–28	34–35	Added: goat
28–30	08–09	Added: building
28–30	23–27	Added: tree
30	16–17	Added: extra story to building

PUZZLE 07

Bora Bora

Bora Bora is a South Pacific island in French Polynesia. Surrounded by a lagoon and a coral reef, it is a popular tourist destination that offers a host of aquatic activities and breath-taking scenery.

01–03	02–04	Added: bird
01–03	26–27	Removed: coral
02–03	14–15	Added: flag
03–05	30–32	Added: boat
03–05	17–19	Changed: water, green to blue
03–06	22–24	Added: cabana
04–05	16–17	Changed: extended rooftop
05	08	Changed: length of roof
05–06	09	Changed: roof, red to green
06–08	17–19	Added: rocky barrier
07	05–06	Changed: size of roof
07–09	28–29	Added: coral
07–09	32-33	Removed: coral
08–09	06–07	Added: spa pool
08–09	08–09	Changed: roof, blue to red
08–09	13–14	Added: tree
08–10	24–26	Added: cabana
08–09	17–20	Added: wharf
09–11	11–12	Changed: size of building
10	14	Changed: height of house
10	17–18	Added: boat
14–16	12–13	Added: round building
14	14–15	Added: coconut tree
14–15	06–07	Added: building
15–16	15–16	Added: beach

15–16	09–10	Added: building
16–18	31–32	Removed: coral
16–18	05–06	Added: tennis court
16–18	12–14	Added: bridge
17–18	11	Added: bus
17–19	20–22	Added: cabana
18–19	15–16	Removed: building
20–22	07	Removed: building
20–22	16–18	Changed: grass to water
21–23	29–30	Added: cabana
22–23	22–23	Removed: cabana
22–24	13–15	Added: building
24–29	18–23	Added: parachutist
25–30	05–9	Added: rocky area
26–27	16–17	Added: cabana
26–27	14–15	Added: bridge
26–27	15–16	Removed: boat
26–27	32–34	Added: dolphin
26–28	24–26	Added: coral
28–29	16–17	Added: tree
28–29	33–34	Added: dolphin
28–30	16–17	Changed: sandbar
28–30	29–31	Added: coral
30	18-19	Removed: island
30	02–04	Added: steps

PUZZLE 08

India

India is famous for its colorful markets, fascinating culture… and chaotic travel in cities! This scene shows vehicles on the road near a busy marketplace. The most popular is the auto-rickshaw taxi—you can see many of these three-wheeled people carriers in the image.

01	21–22	Changed: letter, "H" to "T"
01–03	22–23	Changed: awning, blue to red
01–03	24–25	Changed: awning, green to orange
03–05	15–17	Removed: street light
03	07	Removed: dome
05	03–05	Removed: decoration on dome
05	11–12	Changed: window, blue to brown
06	18	Changed: moped, green to red
06–08	24–25	Changed: awning, red to green
06–09	13–16	Added: tree
06–09	30–32	Changed: rickshaw, yellow to green
07	10–12	Removed: window
08–10	16–17	Added: sign
09	07–08	Removed: turret
09	27	Added: monkey
09–10	26–27	Added: basket
10	30–31	Removed: row of windows
10	35	Removed: man
10–12	04–06	Removed: tree
11–12	10–12	Changed: domed window/balcony
11–12	23–24	Removed: man
12–16	14–21	Added: streetlight
13	14–15	Added: white stripe (detail on building)
13–14	22	Added: green awning over fruit trolley
13–15	32–33	Changed: rickshaw, yellow to green
14	06–07	Added: garlic bulb
14	27–29	Added: woman
15–17	16–17	Added: white car on roof
17	10–11	Changed: window to wall
18–20	04	Added: treetop
18–20	33–35	Changed: direction of motorbike, right to left
19	24–25	Changed: direction of man walking, left to right
19–21	28–30	Changed: rickshaw, yellow to green
21	11–12	Added: elephant
21–22	21–22	Added: man with backpack
21–22	24–25	Changed: roof of rickshaw, black to red
22	06–07	Added: turret
22	22	Changed: shirt, red to blue
24	06–07	Removed: letter "C"
24–25	08	Changed: sign, yellow to blue
24–25	24–26	Removed: two men
25–26	13–15	Added: traffic lights
25–27	17–19	Added: bus
27	13–14	Added: extension to central road barrier
27	24–25	Removed: man
27–28	26–27	Changed: roof of rickshaw, blue to peach
29	08	Changed: billboard reversed
29	14	Added: car
29–30	22–24	Added: man with bicycle
29–30	30	Removed: part of central road barrier

PUZZLE 09

Mexico City

Mexico City is the capital of Mexico and the country's biggest city. Home to more than 21 million people, it is one of the largest metropolitan areas in the world.

01	24–25	Added: window
01–02	14–15	Added: height to building
01–03	14–17	Added: height to building
02–04	06	Added: height to building
04	10	Changed: window
04–05	15	Changed: window cluster
04–06	05–08	Added: dragon
05	25	Added: windows
05–06	21–22	Changed: extended red stripe
07	25	Added: car
07	26–27	Removed: shadow
08	32–34	Removed: skylights
09–11	06–07	Changed: building, red to green
10	11–12	Added: wall
10–12	34–35	Removed: bracing
11	30–31	Changed: awning, yellow to red
11–12	28–29	Removed: square enclosure
11–13	23	Added: extension to roof
12–13	04–05	Changed: height of building
12–16	18–19	Changed: flat roof, brown to green
13–14	10–11	Added: height to building
13–15	17	Changed: rooftop
14	21	Added: x bracing to wall
14–15	16	Added: tree
14–16	06–07	Added: height to building

14–16	25–26	Changed: flat roof, green to red
15–16	22–23	Changed: roof, red to green
15–16	30–32	Added: vents
17–19	06–09	Changed: colors of reflections on building
17–19	12–13	Removed: path (through trees)
18	15	Removed: pillars
18	28	Removed: road markings
19	22–23	Changed: car, red to blue
19	28–29	Added: tree
20	08	Changed: tower
20	10	Added: window
20	11	Changed: front of building
20–27	04–05	Changed: height of mountains
21	27–28	Removed: car
21–22	30–31	Removed: car
23	14–15	Added: fountain
23	17–18	Added: fountain
23	33–34	Changed: car, yellow to green
24	26–27	Changed: banner, green to pink
24	35	Removed: car
26–27	02–03	Added: hot air balloon
26–27	29	Removed: concrete
28–29	26–27	Changed: water feature, yellow to blue
29	15	Removed: purple flowers
29–30	13	Changed: roof, red to green

PUZZLE 10

Colosseum

Built in the center of Rome, Italy, between AD 70–80, the Colosseum is the country's most popular tourist attraction. Made of concrete and stone, and able to hold 80,000 spectators, this giant amphitheater was used primarily for gladiatorial contests and public events. It became a UNESCO World Heritage Site in 1980.

01–02	27–28	Added: branch	17	13	Added: window
01–04	32–35	Added: bush	17	25	Added: branch
04–05	15–16	Removed: people	18–20	12	Changed: wall restored
04–05	30–31	Added: height to wall	19–20	24	Removed: stone blocks
05–06	26–27	Removed: stone	20	13	Added: window
05–10	07–09	Added: cloud	20	15–16	Added: doorway
06	25	Removed: person	20	22–23	Added: railings
06–09	34–35	Changed: stone mound extended	21–22	14–15	Removed: window
06–09	29	Added: stone slab	21–22	19–20	Added: stonework
07–08	20	Added: wall	22–23	26–27	Added: branch
08	27	Added: stone slab	22–28	33–35	Added: bush
09	30–31	Removed: person	23–24	16–17	Added: archway
09–10	26	Added: stone slab	24–25	12–14	Changed: wall extended
11	30–31	Removed: person	24–26	10–11	Removed: cloud
11–12	22–23	Removed: railings	24–26	29–30	Changed: shadow reduced
11–15	05–08	Added: pigeon in flight	25–26	15	Added: height to column
12–13	15–16	Added: height to column	25–26	22–23	Removed: group of people
12–13	26–27	Removed: stone block	26–27	15–16	Removed: window
12–15	34–35	Added: bush	27	24	Removed: people
14	13	Removed: window	27	22–26	Removed: lamppost
14	25	Removed: person	28	26–27	Removed: person
15	19–20	Added: stonework	28–29	03–04	Added: pigeon in flight
15	22	Removed: sign	29	21–23	Removed: railings
15–16	15–16	Added: height to column	30	29	Removed: patch of sunlight
16–17	23	Removed: person	29–30	33–35	Added: ruins

Copacabana

Copacabana Beach lies on the coast of Rio de Janeiro, Brazil. It is famous for its flamboyant New Year's Eve celebrations and 2.5 mile-long promenade.

01–03	12–13	Added: building
01–04	05–09	Added: volcano
02	23–24	Added: person in water
02–05	31–32	Added: rock
03	15–17	Removed: lamppost
04–05	21–22	Added: person jumping
05–06	18–19	Added: lifeguard boat
05–08	13	Added: extension to building
07–08	18	Changed: kiosks, yellow to blue
07–09	32–34	Changed: rock to deckchair
08	07–13	Added: extension to building
09	20	Removed: person
10–11	12–16	Changed: building, white to blue
10–11	21–22	Removed: person
11–12	31–32	Changed: person's legs
12–13	12	Removed: hill top
12–13	27	Removed: person in water
13–14	12	Changed: size of awning
15	21–22	Removed: person
15–17	31–32	Removed: rock
16	20–21	Removed: people
16–17	24–25	Changed: bodyboard, red to blue
16–18	18–19	Added: lifeguard hut
18–19	20–21	Removed: person
19–20	10	Removed: windows
20	06	Added: rooftop room
20	14–18	Removed: lamppost
20–21	20–21	Added: lifeguard flag
20–21	22–23	Changed: swapped people
20–23	09–13	Added: wall mural
21	28	Changed: shorts, red to blue
21	18–19	Added: banner
21	20	Added: person
22	13–14	Removed: glass panels from balcony
22–24	22–24	Added: person
23–24	21	Added: seated person
24–25	09	Added: height to rooftop unit
24–25	16–17	Added: palm tree
24–29	02–04	Added: shooting star
25	10	Added: window
26	23–25	Added: person
26–27	20	Added: sunbather
27	12–18	Added: lamppost
27–28	22–23	Added: person
27–30	06–07	Added: height to hill
28	14–15	Changed: windows
28–29	22–23	Added: trash can
29–30	25	Added: beach ball
29–30	27	Removed: shadow
29–30	21–22	Added: sandcastle

PUZZLE 12

Delhi

Delhi, also known as the National Capital Territory of India, is India's largest metropolitan area and the world's second most populous city with over two million residents.

01–02	21–22	Added: turban
01–02	22–25	Removed: bag
01–03	26–27	Changed: headscarf, blue to orange
01–04	34–35	Removed: woman
02–03	01–04	Removed: speaker
03–04	08–09	Added: snake
03	11–14	Added: sign
04–08	08–09	Changed: length of beam
05–06	17–19	Removed: person
05–09	31–32	Added: umbrella
05–08	34	Added: manhole cover
06–07	01–02	Changed: window blue to pink
07–08	11	Changed: "R" to "B"
07–08	18–21	Added: person
08–09	25–26	Added: hat
10–11	17–18	Changed: vest, red to blue
10–11	21–23	Changed: shirt, orange to blue
10–11	31–35	Added: scarf
11–12	05	Changed: "W" to "V"
11–12	10	Changed: direction of arrow
12–14	19–20	Changed: metal green to orange
13–17	01–02	Added: sign
13	14–15	Removed: person
13	28–29	Removed: pattern from scarf
14	11–12	Added: goat

15	17	Added: dog
16–17	04–05	Removed: part of wall
16	08–09	Added: air conditioner
16–17	13	Added: parasol
17–18	16–17	Added: box
18–19	04–05	Removed: green box
18–20	24	Added: alligator
19–21	14–15	Changed: metal, blue to green
19–20	19–20	Changed: shirt, yellow to blue
20–21	01–01	Removed: tangled wire
20	05–07	Removed: top of post
20	09	Changed: box, red to green
21–22	19–25	Added: person
22–26	23–25	Added: bag
23–35	18–24	Changed: direction of man
24–25	06–08	Added: sign
25	01–02	Changed: wall, yellow to green
25–26	14–15	Changed: direction of symbol
25–26	16–17	Added: framed picture
26–27	02–04	Added: power line loop
17–28	18	Added: heart carving
26–28	27–28	Removed: helmet
28–29	06–08	Changed: sheet, pink to white
28–29	24	Added: sunglasses
28–30	29–32	Added: bag

PUZZLE 13

Palace of Versailles

King Louis XIII constructed a hunting lodge in the village of Versailles in 1624. His son and successor, King Louis XIV, transformed the lodge into a palace, and moved the court and government there in 1682. The palace now contains the "Hall of Mirrors," the famous room where the Treaty of Versailles was signed in 1919.

01	08–09	Removed: statue
01–04	33–34	Added: tree top
02	09–10	Added: column
02	15–18	Removed: arch
03	12	Added: stone vase
03	18–20	Added: topiary
03–04	26–27	Removed: topiary
03–04	29–30	Added: topiary
04	12	Added: stone vase
05	07	Removed: roof decoration
06	08	Removed: window
06–07	19–20	Removed: topiary
07–08	23–24	Removed: topiary
07–08	31–34	Removed: topiary corner
08	24–25	Added: height to conifer
09	32–33	Removed: branch of conifer
09–11	07–09	Added: seagull
10	11–12	Removed: window
10–11	14–16	Removed: arch
10–11	27–30	Added: width to shaped grass
10–11	31–32	Removed: path cutout
11	11	Removed: chimney
11–12	21–22	Removed: topiary
12–13	14–15	Removed: trellis window
12–13	18–19	Removed: topiary edging

13–14	11–12	Removed: window
13–14	21–23	Changed: plant
13–14	23–24	Changed: moved topiary edging to left
13–15	27–28	Changed: path extended
14	11–12	Added: height to chimney
15	12	Removed: window
15–21	34–35	Added: tree top
16–17	17–20	Added: conifer
17–18	22–23	Removed: topiary
17–21	28–31	Added: tent
19–21	25–26	Added: grass
20	24	Removed: end of spiral, now grassed over
22–23	12	Removed: window
23–24	14–15	Removed: trellis window
23–24	27–28	Removed: square from grass
24	19–23	Added: conifer
24–26	24–25	Changed: moved topiary edging to right
25–26	23–24	Removed: topiary
26	14–16	Added: stone column
26–28	20–21	Added: red boat
27–28	14–16	Added: doorway
27–28	22–24	Added: fisherman
28–30	20–22	Changed: topiary to tree top
29–30	15–19	Added: height to conifer
30	23–24	Added: topiary

PUZZLE 14

Potala Palace

The Potala Palace lies on the Red Hill in Lhasa, Tibet. It is comprised of the Red Palace and the White Palace; the former contains a complex of libraries and Buddhist chapels, the latter was the living quarters of the Dalai Lama until 1959. Today it is a UNESCO World Heritage Site.

01	15–16	Added: skier	15	28–29	Changed: globe enlarged
01–02	18	Added: extension to building	15–16	17–19	Changed: building extended
01–02	26–27	Changed: grid on window	15–16	29	Changed: panel, blue to black
01–04	24–25	Changed: stripes reversed	16	11–12	Removed: banner
01–06	02–09	Added: cloud	16–18	07–09	Changed: building, yellow to red
02–03	10–11	Changed: wall, yellow to red	17–18	19–21	Added: tree
02–03	14–15	Added: cracks	17–22	18	Added: wall
03–04	20–21	Removed: window	18	30	Changed: direction of arrow, from right to left
04–05	24	Added: wooden strut	18–19	09–10	Removed: window
04–05	26–31	Added: man	20–28	12–13	Removed: wall
05–06	24	Added: wooden strut	21	07	Changed: window, red to orange
06	19	Added: window	21	27	Changed: jacket, red to fluorescent yellow
06–07	06–07	Removed: roof decoration	22	05–06	Added: height to roof decoration
06–07	18	Added: brick edging	22–23	23–24	Added: window
06–09	22–23	Changed: size of eaves	22–25	29–32	Added: deer
08–09	16–17	Removed: tree	23	27–28	Removed: person
08–10	06–07	Changed: banner, yellow to red	23–24	09	Added: red window dressing
09	05–06	Changed: flag, from furled to flying	23–25	25–26	Removed: window
09–13	20–22	Changed: tree, now bigger	23–26	14–22	Added: tree
10	13	Added: window	27–30	27–28	Changed: flowers, pink to green
11	10–11	Added: window	28–29	18–19	Added: rock climber
12	06	Changed: window to plaque	28–30	09–12	Added: overhanging window
12–14	28–29	Added: bench	28–30	16–17	Removed: tree
13–15	05–06	Added: flags	30	13–14	Added: ice cave
15	13–16	Added: drainpipe	30	21–23	Added: decorative pillar

PUZZLE 15

Dubai

Dubai is the main city and one of the seven principalities that comprise the United Arab Emirates. It lies within the Arabian Desert on the coast of the Persian Gulf.

01	08–10	Changed: height of building
01–03	17–18	Changed: wall, brown to green
01–28	28	Changed: road sign, blue to red
01–02	32–34	Removed: truck
01–02	34–35	Changed: expanded road
02–04	02–05	Removed: crane
03	08–12	Removed: building section
03	30–32	Removed: lamppost
03–04	21	Removed: vehicles
04–05	08–09	Removed: elevator shaft
04–06	19–20	Changed: roof, red to blue
09–11	10–13	Changed: height of building
10–11	35	Removed: road marking
11–12	17	Changed: height of building
11–12	21	Changed: extended window
11–12	29–30	Removed: windows
12–13	11–12	Removed: building section
12–15	14–15	Changed: height of building
13–14	08	Removed: building top
13–14	33–34	Removed: tall window
14–15	18–19	Removed: trees
14–17	20	Changed: roof, red to green
14–15	28	Changed: pool, blue to green
15–16	19	Changed: height of building
16	13–14	Removed: dark square

16	27–28	Changed: size of balcony
16–17	34–35	Removed: tree and grass
17	07–08	Removed: roof antenna
17–18	19–20	Added: trees and bushes
17–18	28–29	Added: domed tower
17–18	32–33	Removed: hut and bushes
18–19	05–08	Changed: height of building
18–19	12–16	Changed: height of building
18–20	21–22	Changed: height of building
21–22	03–04	Removed: roof section
21–22	17	Removed: opening
21–22	20	Changed: extended roof
21–22	25	Added: balcony
21–22	27–28	Added: windows
21–22	32–33	Removed: cabin
25–27	22–23	Added: extended building
27	08–11	Removed: building
27	13–14	Changed: height of building
27	21–22	Added: bushes
27–28	25–26	Removed: yellow van
28–29	17–18	Added: trees
28–29	26–27	Removed: truck
28–30	34–35	Removed: bar over road
29	23–25	Added: extended median strip
29–30	26	Changed: extended sign

PUZZLE 16

St. Basil's Cathedral

The Cathedral of Vasily the Blessed, better known as Saint Basil's Cathedral, is a museum and former church situated in Moscow's Red Square. Its construction was ordered by Ivan the Terrible to commemorate the capture of Kazan from the Mongols, and was completed in 1560.

01	29–30	Changed: height of window
02–03	23–24	Added: flying swan
02–03	27–29	Added: pointed roof
05–07	33–24	Added: dancer
07–08	15–16	Changed: tiles, red to purple
07	19–20	Added: arch windows
07	21–22	Removed: circle from archway
08–09	21	Removed: holes from archway
09–09	23–25	Changed: triangle, red to blue
09	31	Removed: archway
09	33–34	Removed: people
10	18–20	Removed: striped spire
11–13	23–34	Changed: wall, green to red
11–12	25	Changed: arch, red to blue
12–14	04–07	Changed: domed spire, gold to silver
12–13	07	Added: arch details to tower
12–13	11–12	Added: arch detail
12–13	15	Removed: star from archway
12–13	17	Changed: circle, red to purple
12	22–23	Removed: arched window
12	30	Changed: column detail
14	19–20	Changed: height of window
14	22	Removed: cream square
14–15	27–28	Removed: arched window
14–15	33–34	Added: dancer

15–19	14–18	Changed: roof, red to blue
15–17	28–32	Added: bare tree
16–17	19	Removed: diamonds from tower
16–17	23–25	Changed: triangle, red to green
17	30–31	Changed: square, red to purple
17–18	20–21	Changed: triangle arch, red to green
19–29	04–08	Added: helicopter
19	30–31	Removed: white rectangle
20–21	12–13	Added: flag
20–21	16–19	Changed: roof swirl, green to blue
20	22–23	Removed: arched window
20–21	24	Changed: arch, red to purple
20–21	25–26	Removed: window
21	28	Added: arched window
21	30–31	Removed: window
21–24	33–34	Removed: vehicles
22–30	13–35	Added: lamppost
22–24	24–25	Removed: roof section
24–25	26–27	Added: attic window
24–27	28–29	Changed: height of building
26–27	31–34	Added: polar bear
27–28	20–21	Added: windows in spire
27–28	26–27	Changed: archway, half blocked
28–29	27–32	Added: bare tree
28–29	33	Added: side entrance

PUZZLE 17

Stockholm

Founded in the thirteenth century, Sweden's capital spreads over fourteen islands to the coast of the Baltic Sea. It is the seat of the Swedish government and its monarchy, and is an important global city.

01–02	19–21	Changed: length of roof
01–03	13	Removed: dock
03	26–27	Removed: window
03–04	11–12	Added: buildings
03–04	17–19	Changed: length of building
04–05	20	Changed: roof, red to blue
04–05	26	Removed: window
06–09	04–05	Added: goose
06–07	12–13	Removed: buildings
07–08	15	Changed: roof, orange to green
07–09	21–22	Changed: wall, red to blue
07–08	23	Removed: window
08–09	11	Removed: building
08–10	16–17	Changed: roof, red to gray
08	24	Added: window
08–09	28–29	Removed: window
09–10	30–31	Removed: vehicle
10–14	12–13	Removed: cruise ship
11–12	17–19	Changed: building, green to purple
11–12	23	Added: window
11	24	Removed: window
11	26–27	Removed: window
11–12	27–30	Added: tree
12–13	15–16	Changed: roof, green to orange
12–15	25	Changed: roof, red to green

13	27	Removed: window
14	28	Added: window
14–16	18–19	Changed: wall, red to green
15–17	28–29	Added: scaffold
17–18	11–12	Removed: buildings
17–18	19–20	Changed: tower, blue to red
17–19	22–23	Removed: scaffold from roof
19–20	31	Removed: ring
20–22	15	Removed: building
22–23	14	Removed: boat
23	10–11	Removed: tower
23–24	18–19	Removed: tower on roof
24–25	29	Removed: shadow
25	15–16	Removed: church window
25	16–17	Removed: church clock
25	22	Removed: window
25	30	Added: ring
27–28	22	Removed: window
27–29	24	Changed: wall, brown to blue
28–29	12–13	Removed: background building
29–30	11–12	Removed: building
29–30	18	Removed: roof section
30	21	Removed: window
30	24–27	Added: tree
30	29	Removed: ring

PUZZLE 18

Venice

This Italian city is a very popular tourist destination. It is famed for its great beauty and large number of bridges, canals, and churches. The photograph shows the Doge's Palace (Palazzo Ducale), which dates from the twelfth century.

01	17–18	Removed: balustrade
01	22–23	Changed: shirt, red to green
01–02	25	Changed: stroller, red to green
03–04	04–07	Added: arched window
03–04	23	Added: chair
04–06	31–34	Changed: shorts, brown to blue
05–06	18	Removed: balustrade
06–07	05	Added: drainpipe
06–08	27–29	Added: pigeon
07	07–08	Added: circular window
07–08	01–03	Added: pigeon
07–08	24–25	Added: metal chair
07–08	26–27	Removed: pigeon
08	14–16	Added: relief sculpture
09–10	21	Removed: black sign
09–11	26–29	Added: beggar with straw hat
10–11	11–13	Removed: arched window
10–11	17–18	Removed: interior of archway
11	07–08	Removed: triangular decoration on roof
11–12	09–10	Removed: circular window
12	16–17	Changed: relief sculpture
12	18–19	Removed: column
12–13	34–35	Removed: bottom of cardigan
14–15	17–18	Added: airplane
14–15	25	Added: blue hat

15	29	Removed: red ticket from hand
15–16	25–26	Removed: plastic bag
16–17	21	Added: beach ball
16–17	23–24	Changed: shirt, yellow to blue
17–18	25–26	Changed: jacket, beige to blue
18	20	Removed: light from lamppost
18–19	32–33	Added: white path
19–20	16–19	Changed: tower extended
19–20	27–28	Added: pigeon
20	24–25	Removed: camera from tourist
20–21	14–15	Changed: direction of lion, from left to right
20–21	19–20	Removed: tower
21	24–25	Added: chair
21–23	34–35	Removed: white paving stones
22–30	08–14	Removed: cloud
22	21	Changed: statue, white to blue
25–27	14–16	Added: pigeon
26	25	Removed: logo from shirt
26–27	31	Added: logo to shirt
27	20–21	Removed: red pole
28	19–20	Added: pigeon
28	21	Removed: black sign
28–29	25–26	Removed: camera strap from tourist
28–30	29–34	Changed: shirt, purple to green
29	21	Removed: trees from behind building

PUZZLE 19

Fort Lauderdale

Fort Lauderdale is located in the southern tip of Florida. Its nickname is "Venice of America" due to the rivers that run through it, and its proximity to the ocean. It is a very popular tourist destination, enjoying sunshine and fair weather all year round.

01–02	05	Removed: boat
01–06	31–32	Removed: wave
02–03	17–18	Added: height to building
03–04	23–24	Removed: tree
04	05–06	Removed: structure on bridge
04–06	13–15	Added: tree
04–06	21	Changed: awning, red to green
05	24	Removed: shadow of tree
06	03–05	Added: lighthouse
06	18–19	Changed: structure on roof
06	25	Changed: umbrella, blue to green
06–07	06–07	Removed: mooring
06–10	32–34	Added: shark
07	09–12	Added: yellow panel
07	24	Removed: shadow of tree
07–10	21	Changed: awning, blue to red
07–11	07–08	Removed: boats
08	25–26	Removed: white box
08–09	01–03	Added: extension to apartment block
09–10	19	Changed: car, orange to green
10–12	04–05	Changed: two buildings to one building
11	13–14	Removed: truck
11	24–25	Added: lifeguard's tower
11–14	19–21	Added: baseball diamond
14	04–05	Added: extension to mooring

14–16	22	Changed: awning, orange to green
14–18	06	Added: speedboat and wake
15	20–21	Added: skylight
16	13–14	Added: car
16	23–24	Changed: height of bollard
16–17	23	Changed: position of car, moved forward
17	16	Changed: arrow road marking reversed
19–20	17	Removed: white wall
20	02	Added: height to dome window
20–21	03–04	Added: roof to square structure
20–21	19	Added: balcony
22	21	Removed: window
22–23	16–17	Added: extension to building
22–26	03–04	Added: extension to building
23	25–26	Removed: shadow of tree
23–24	26	Added: umbrella
24–25	16–17	Added: square arch over pool
24–25	18–19	Added: extension to greenery
24–27	19	Removed: fence
25–27	24	Changed: lower part of bus, red to blue
27–28	04	Removed: small structure
27–28	06–16	Added: white column to building
28	23–24	Removed: palm tree
29–30	27	Added: tent
30	20	Added: logo

PUZZLE 20

Old Jerusalem

The Old City is a walled area within modern Jerusalem that contains sacred sites for all three Abrahamic religions, including the Temple Mount (Judaism), the Church of the Holy Sepulchre (Christianity), and the Dome of the Rock (Islam).

01–02	11–16	Added: palm tree	16	20–22	Removed: window
01–02	18–19	Added: window	17	13	Added: window
01–02	24	Changed: height of wall	17–21	34–35	Removed: dome
01–02	31–33	Added: satellite dish	18	17	Added: window
03	12–13	Removed: tower	19–20	16	Removed: barrel
04–05	13–14	Added: satellite dish	19–20	22–23	Added: cylinder
04	15–16	Added: window	20	15	Removed: window
05	15–16	Removed: window	20–22	30–32	Removed: object
05–06	26–27	Changed: length of wall	20–21	10–11	Removed: antenna
05–08	14	Changed: cover, blue to red	20–23	15–16	Added: dome
06	16	Changed: door, green to orange	21	14	Removed: window
07	19	Removed: window	21–22	24	Added: window
07	31–33	Added: window	22–23	18–19	Removed: window
08–09	12–13	Removed: chimney	23	09	Removed: window
12–13	12–13	Removed: tree	23–24	10–11	Added: window
12–15	16–17	Changed: height of wall	24–26	21–23	Added: satellite dish
12–13	20–21	Changed: height of window	25–26	08–12	Removed: antenna
12	23–24	Added: window	25–26	17	Changed: roof, red to green
13–14	18–19	Added: cylinder and panel	25	18–19	Removed: window
13	35	Removed: small window	27	13	Added: satellite dish
14	12–13	Added: satellite dish	27–28	14–15	Removed: window
14	14	Removed: cylinder	27–28	33–35	Removed: cylinder
14–18	25–32	Added: palm tree	29–30	28–32	Changed: height of wall
15–19	15	Changed: height of building	29–30	12–13	Added: palm tree
16–17	11–12	Removed: satellite dish	30	34–35	Removed: window

PUZZLE 21

Étretat

Étretat is a town situated on the coast of northwestern France. It is famous for its arch-shaped cliffs and is a popular tourist destination. Many of the cliffs were made famous by Impressionist painters such as Claude Monet.

01	01–02	Changed: length of building
02–03	16	Added: chimney
03–04	03–04	Added: wing to building
03–04	12–13	Added: chimney
03–05	16–18	Added: pipes
03–04	18–19	Removed: poster
04–06	11	Removed: pattern
05	15	Removed: door
06–07	22–25	Removed: lamppost
08–10	15–17	Added: building extension
09	21–22	Added: waste container
09–10	23–24	Changed: order of people
09–10	27–28	Changed: size of person
10	04–07	Added: tower
10	10	Added: window
11–12	08	Changed: awning, blue to purple
11–12	11–12	Added: banner
11–12	16–17	Added: tractor
11–12	24–25	Added: skateboarder
11–12	01–02	Removed: umbrella
12	07–08	Changed: closed window shutters
12–13	14	Changed: opened umbrella
12–13	15	Removed: waste container
13–14	02	Removed: "HOTEL"
13–15	11–12	Changed: cover, red to white

13–14	19–20	Removed: roof
14	14	Changed: flag, green to red
15	06	Removed: dormer window
15	08–10	Added: banner
16	12–14	Changed: direction of banner
16–17	15–16	Added: stairs
17	10	Removed: removed car
18	06–07	Changed: window frames
20–21	10	Changed: flag, blue to orange
21–26	01–05	Added: hot air balloon
21–22	06–07	Removed: swing set
21–22	08	Added: boat
22–24	13	Changed: boat, red to blue
23	14	Removed: sign
23	23	Changed: direction of person
23–24	28–29	Removed: person
24	10	Added: concrete barrier
24	11	Changed: boat, blue to green
25	06–07	Added: building
25	15–16	Added: life-preserver
26–27	11–12	Added: tent
27–28	06	Removed: tunnel
29–30	06–07	Removed: shack
29–30	21–22	Added: boat
30	27	Added: person

PUZZLE 22

Hagia Sophia

Hagia Sophia (from Greek, meaning "Holy Wisdom") was constructed in AD 537 as an Eastern Orthodox cathedral. Between 1204 and 1261 it became a Roman Catholic cathedral, then from 1453 to 1931 it was converted into a mosque. In 1935, it was secularized and opened as a museum.

01	05–06	Added: height to stained glass window
01–03	08–10	Added: decorative border
03–04	02–03	Changed: angel's wing extended
03–05	22–23	Added: extended balcony
05	26–27	Changed: panel, gray to gold
05	30–32	Changed: archway extended
06	19–21	Removed: chandelier from archway
06–07	30–31	Removed: visitor
07–08	09–10	Changed: décor restored
07–10	32–34	Added: chandelier
08	15–16	Changed: window opened
08–09	16–18	Added: pigeon in flight
08–09	28–30	Added: column
09	23	Removed: star
10	28–30	Added: column
10–11	11	Added: decorative diamond
10–11	23–24	Added: religious icon
10–11	27–28	Changed: panel extended
12	12–13	Removed: triangular decoration from circle
12	31–32	Changed: jacket, gray to yellow
12	35	Removed: visitor
12–15	25–26	Added: plain cream tiles
13	23–24	Removed: pattern from window, now plain glass
13–14	09–10	Removed: décor
13–15	27–28	Changed: wall raised

14	22	Removed: plaque
14–15	16–17	Added: window
14–15	18–19	Removed: plaque
15–16	01–02	Changed: window covered
15–16	19–21	Added: stained glass pattern to plain window
17–18	11–12	Added: arched window
18	23–24	Changed: window covered
19–20	06–07	Changed: line of décor restored
19–20	27–28	Added: height to doorway
19–20	24	Added: layers of gold décor
19–21	18	Added: line of script
20–22	30–32	Removed: chandelier
21–22	12–13	Changed: damage restored
22	23–24	Added: religious icon
22	27–28	Added: marble panel
22–23	13–16	Removed: line of décor
23–24	18	Removed: window
23–24	32–33	Removed: panel in front of opening
25–26	05–06	Added: face
25–27	23–28	Added: shield
27–28	30–32	Removed: chandelier
28	23–25	Added: religious icon
28–29	17–21	Added: column
29	27–28	Removed: dark pattern from marble
30	35	Removed: visitor

PUZZLE 23

Ho Chi Minh City

Vietnam's largest city, and home to nine million residents, Ho Chi Minh (formerly Saigon) is the economic center of the country, but not the capital city. Popular tourist destinations include Dong Khoi Road, and the famous Cho Lon and Cho Ben Thanh markets.

01	11–12	Added: white exhaust to truck	18–20	06–08	Added: lamppost
01–02	07–09	Added: car	18–20	18–19	Removed: motorcyclist
01–02	10–11	Added: tank on truck	19–20	01–02	Changed: fence, white to brown
01–03	23–29	Added: foliage to tree	19–20	24–25	Added: row of fans to roof of bus
01–04	11–14	Changed: truck, red to blue	19–21	26–28	Changed: panel, blue to orange
03	02	Changed: symbol on flag	20–21	31–33	Added: cyclist
03	17–18	Changed: shirt, red to blue	21	03	Changed: shirt, red to brown
03	21–22	Changed: flag, now draped in front of wires	21–22	24	Changed: stripe, red to black
05	09–10	Removed: road marking	21–22	35	Changed: star, yellow to blue
06–10	09–10	Added: sinkhole	22–23	19–20	Changed: shirt, blue to orange
07–09	14–15	Changed: central road barrier extended	22–23	26–27	Added: round roof vent
08–12	07–09	Added: puddle	22–24	01–05	Changed: direction of motorcyclist, left to right
09	06	Added: bush	24–25	13–14	Removed: island
09–11	16–17	Changed: road marking, now unbroken	24–25	27–28	Added: bus surfer
10–11	29–30	Added: dark gray paving tile	25	18	Removed: puddle
12	14–15	Added: logo	26	11–12	Removed: logo
12–14	33–35	Removed: tree	26	14	Changed: symbol on flag to Pacman
12–13	05–06	Removed: roof antenna	26–27	15–17	Added: man
10–13	06–07	Removed: flag	26–27	31–32	Removed: road marking
13–16	16–18	Removed: road marking (stripe of crossing)	26–28	03–05	Added: small palm tree
14–15	11–13	Removed: foliage from back of bike	26–29	19–21	Added: motorcyclist
13–15	18–20	Changed: back of vehicle	26–30	07–08	Removed: white wire
14–16	32–33	Added: patterned paving tiles	27–29	13–15	Added: tree
14–17	22–26	Removed: back of bus	28–30	08–15	Added: flagpole
15–16	01	Removed: person	29–30	07–08	Added: motorcycle

PUZZLE 24: United States Capitol

| 01 | 02 | 03 | 04 | 05 | 06 | 07 | 08 | 09 | 10 | 11 | 12 | 13 | 14 | 15 | 16 | 17 | 18 | 19 | 20 | 21 | 22 | 23 | 24 | 25 | 26 | 27 | 28 | 29 | 30 |

PUZZLE 24

United States Capitol

The United States Capitol, perched atop Capitol Hill in the National Mall, Washington, D.C., is the powerhouse of the United States Congress. Washington, D.C. was built around the Capitol, which is positioned at the meeting point of the District's four quadrants.

01	19–20	Added: extra story to building
01	22–23	Removed: window
01–02	13–14	Deleted: white structure
02	31–33	Removed: lamppost
02	35	Removed: road marking
02–03	18–19	Removed: windows
02–04	15–16	Added: white section to building
03–04	34	Removed: road marking (arrow)
04–05	30–31	Removed: road marking
04–05	19–20	Added: tower
04–08	33–35	Added: tree top
05	23	Removed: windows
05	32	Removed: road marking
05–07	16–18	Added: top story of building extended
06	27–29	Removed: post
06–07	16	Removed: windows
06–08	29–30	Added: pigeon in flight
07–09	12–13	Removed: building
08	28	Removed: pedestrians crossing road
08–09	18–22	Changed: building, blue to brown
09	26	Removed: car
09–10	12–14	Added: building extended
09–11	31–33	Added: branches
10	17–18	Added: section to building
11–12	27–28	Removed: car

14	14–15	Added: tree
14–15	34–35	Added: gutter extension
15–17	11	Removed: building
16–18	24–26	Added: trees
19–21	28–29	Added: chimney
20	19–20	Added: window
20–21	17–18	Changed: roof, red to green
20–21	21	Removed: window
21–23	14–15	Changed: building section removed
20–23	11–12	Removed: buildings
20–26	31–33	Changed: rooftop, red to green
22–23	29–31	Removed: window
22–25	23	Changed: surface, red to green
23	19–20	Removed: plaque
23	24–25	Removed: window
24–25	27–28	Removed: roof vent
25–28	24–25	Added: height to building extension
26–28	05–07	Added: pigeon in flight
27–28	12–14	Added: extension to building
27–28	20–21	Removed: plaque
27–28	23–24	Removed: window
27–28	29–30	Changed: height of window reduced
28–30	11	Added: building
28–30	26–27	Added: chimney
29–30	31–34	Added: chimney

PUZZLE 25

Santorini

Santorini is an island situated approximately 120 miles (200 km) from the coast of Greece in the southern Aegean Sea. It contains a vast central lagoon surrounded by cliffs on three sides.

01–03	11–15	Changed: extended cliff
01–03	20–21	Removed: building
02–04	07–10	Added: tree
04	30	Added: window
05–06	17–18	Added: bush
05	28–29	Removed: window
05–06	31–32	Removed: pillar
06–07	24	Removed: lounge chairs
06–08	34–35	Removed: lounge chair
07–08	32–33	Removed: person in doorway
08–09	05–06	Added: seagull
08–09	08	Removed: bush
08–09	25	Removed: window
09–10	20–21	Added: window
10	26–27	Removed: stone wall
11–13	20	Changed: extended wall
13–14	17	Changed: extended wall
13	24–25	Added: window
14	11	Removed: window
16–17	09	Removed: window
16–17	19	Removed: hole above door
16–18	26–28	Changed: building extended
16–17	33–34	Removed: opening
17–19	05	Changed: windmill roof
17–19	13	Removed: greenery from wall

17	15	Added: window
18	18–19	Changed: height of door
19	12	Added: window
20–21	14–15	Added: tower
20	34–35	Removed: window
21	05–06	Added: arch
22–25	15–19	Added: tree
22	25–26	Removed: door
22	30	Removed: window
23–24	10–11	Added: boarded window
23–25	13–14	Changed: extended railing
24	03	Removed: window from windmill
24–25	29	Removed: window
25–26	03–04	Removed: building
25–27	32–34	Changed: height of wall
26	10	Added: window
26–28	22–24	Changed: width of cave
27–28	07	Changed: arch
27	11	Removed: blue gate
28–29	33–34	Changed: height of window
29–30	01–02	Removed: roof
29–30	03–04	Removed: window
29–30	12–14	Added: wall
29–30	18–23	Added: tree
29–30	25–26	Removed: cave

PUZZLE 26

River Thames

Home to twenty-five species of fish and forty-five locks, the meandering River Thames is 215 miles (346 km) long and travels from the Cotswolds, south central England, straight into the heart of London. The Thames' first crossing was London Bridge, a wooden pontoon built 2,000 years ago by Roman settlers.

01–02	03–08	Added: the Shard building
01–04	11	Added: arched bridge
01–04	27–23	Added: section to bridge
02	29	Added: biplane
03	23–24	Removed: tower
04	28–30	Changed: façade of tower of bridge
03–04	25	Added: baseball cap
04–05	05–06	Added: windmill
04–05	16	Added: boat
05–06	12–13	Added: height to apartment block
05–06	23	Added: extra story to building
05–06	25–26	Changed: tower of London Bridge to Big Ben
05–07	31	Added: bus
05–14	28–32	Changed: bridge suspension, blue to pink
06–09	05–06	Removed: body of water
06–14	32–34	Removed: shadow of bridge
09	08–09	Changed: stripes on apartment block, yellow to blue
09–10	22–23	Added: extension to wharf
09–10	24–25	Added: boat
09–11	18–20	Changed: building, green to brown
09–13	16–17	Added: pool of water
10–11	13–15	Added: church
10–11	21–22	Added: scaffolding
12–13	04	Added: height to building

13–14	21	Added: sandbar
14–15	09–10	Removed: gap between buildings
14–15	28–29	Added: length to boat
14–15	35	Changed: grass, green to brown
15–16	20	Added: boarding bridge
15–16	22	Changed: boat, blue to red
15–17	32–33	Changed: bridge suspension, blue to green
16	34–35	Removed: tree
16–17	08	Removed: indent in building
17–18	16	Added: extra story to building
18–19	33	Removed: vehicle
18–21	10–11	Removed: white building
19	26–27	Added: chimney
20–21	30–33	Added: tower
20–21	34–35	Added: extension to building
22–25	23–24	Added: extra story to building
23–24	15–16	Changed: length of wharf reduced
24	23	Removed: yellow buoy
24–25	33–34	Added: section to building site
25–26	17–18	Changed: direction of boat
27	31–32	Changed: building, red to blue
27–28	28	Changed: roof, green to red
28	16	Added: whale jumping out of water
29–30	18–19	Added: yacht
29–30	24–27	Removed: arm of crane
30	29–30	Changed: roof, gray to white

PUZZLE 27

Persepolis

Persepolis, which now lies in modern Iran, was the ceremonial capital of the First Persian Empire. Although the city was partially destroyed by Alexander the Great, many impressive buildings constructed of gray marble have been excavated.

01–02	15–16	Removed: sign
01–04	26–27	Changed: height of wall
02–03	07–08	Removed: tree
02–03	18–19	Added: stone
02–03	21	Added: stone
02–03	22–23	Removed: stones
02–04	31–33	Removed: scaffold
03–06	13–14	Changed: holes
03–05	14–15	Added: statues
04–05	16–18	Changed: doorway opened
04–05	20–21	Changed: height of column
05–07	25–27	Removed: damage to stone
05–08	33–35	Added: pillars
06	20	Changed: coat, red to green
07–08	16	Removed: person
08–09	21–22	Added: stone
09	13–15	Removed: post
09–10	21–22	Removed: stones
09–10	23	Added: stone
10–11	17	Removed: bench
10–13	25–30	Added: door ornamentation
11	05–10	Added: column
12–13	13–18	Added: door statue
15–16	28–29	Removed: stone
16–18	20–21	Changed: stonework
16–18	34	Removed: wall section
17	15–16	Removed: person
17–20	15	Changed: top of doorway
17–18	17–18	Removed: stone
18–19	28–29	Removed: stonework
19–20	20	Removed: stones
19	24–26	Removed: stone
20	13–16	Removed: post
21–22	05–10	Removed: column
21–22	21–22	Removed: stones
23–24	16–18	Changed: doorway opened
23–24	19	Added: stone
23–28	32–33	Removed: stone inset
24	14	Removed: people
24–25	08–10	Added: column
24–25	15	Added: stone head
24–26	25–26	Removed: damage to stone
25	20–21	Removed: person
25–26	23	Removed: stone
26–27	04	Removed: top of column
27–29	15–19	Removed: doorway
27–28	23–24	Added: stone
28	05–09	Changed: height of column
28	20–21	Changed: coat, red to blue
29–30	25–26	Added: stone column

PUZZLE 28

Peru

The Republic of Peru is a country in the west of South America, bordering Bolivia, Brazil, Chile, Colombia, Ecuador, and the Pacific Ocean. While 60 percent of Peru may be covered in Amazon rainforests, the country also boasts very beautiful coastal areas.

01–02	14–15	Changed: height of building
01–02	22–25	Added: tree
01–02	29–31	Added: tree
01–04	33–35	Added: tree
03–09	03–06	Added: seagull
02–03	20	Removed: vehicle
02–03	25	Removed: person
03–04	26	Removed: wrapped paraglider
04–06	09–10	Removed: building
04–05	18	Removed: path
04–05	19	Added: vehicle
04	29	Changed: shirts, red to blue
05–06	33–34	Removed: waste container
06–07	20–22	Added: tree
06–07	31–32	Added: path section
07	14–15	Removed: top of tree
07–08	32–33	Removed: path section
08–11	28–29	Changed: size of shadow
09–10	10–11	Removed: top of building
09–11	24–26	Changed: parachute, orange to blue
09–10	32–33	Changed: length of block
11–12	07–09	Changed: height of building
11–14	32–33	Added: greenery
12	29	Removed: shadow
14–16	24–25	Changed: graphic, blue to red

15–16	18	Changed: height of wall
16–17	20	Added: shadow
18–19	22–23	Removed: shadow
19–20	10–13	Changed: height of building
19	25	Removed: person
20	17–18	Changed: sculpture, red to purple
20–22	19–21	Changed: greenery to dirt
21–23	31–32	Added: mud
22	14–15	Changed: height of sculpture
22–23	23–24	Added: seagull
23–28	03–10	Added: paraglider
23	15	Removed: small building
24	21–22	Removed: vehicle
25–27	14–15	Changed: extended beach
25	25	Removed: vehicle
25–26	15–17	Added: tree
27	25	Added: bushes
27–28	33–34	Added: seagull
28–30	11–13	Added: paraglider
28–30	18–21	Added: paraglider
28	19–20	Removed: shadow
28–29	22–23	Removed: vehicle
28–29	25	Removed: vehicle
28	30	Added: vehicle
29–30	15–16	Removed: paraglider

PUZZLE 29

Petra

Petra is an ancient city built from rose-colored stone that was rediscovered in 1812 by Swiss Explorer Johann Ludwig. Today it is Jordan's most popular tourist attraction.

01	06–11	Added: stone wall
01–02	24	Removed: bush
01–02	27–32	Added: plant
01–02	31–32	Changed: shadow
01–03	18–23	Added: plant
01–03	25–27	Added: fox
01–11	31–34	Added: skull
02–03	10–11	Removed: shadow
02–07	01–07	Changed: mountain extended
03	20–21	Added: shadow
04–05	08–14	Changed: width of stonework
04–05	16–22	Added: stone column
05	24–25	Removed: corner of bench
06–07	19–20	Changed: window open
06–08	22–24	Removed: person
07–11	26–28	Changed: shirt, red to green
08–12	05–07	Changed: height of roof
09–10	12–13	Changed: shadow
09–10	15–22	Added: stone column
09–11	10–11	Changed: height of stonework
11–13	23–24	Changed: coat, yellow to orange
12–14	05–07	Removed: stone section
13–16	09–10	Changed: stonework
13–16	16–18	Changed: height of door
14–15	14	Added: stonework

14–15	22	Removed: person
14–15	26–27	Added: skull
14–18	33–34	Changed: shape of shadow
16–18	26	Removed: shadow
18–21	07–09	Changed: height of stonework
18–20	12	Added: stonework
18–20	16–22	Added: stone column
19	13–15	Changed: window open
19–22	24–28	Changed: shirt, green to red
20–24	03–05	Added: vulture
20–21	23–24	Removed: person
20–21	34–35	Removed: leaves
21–22	21–23	Added: camel
22–23	09	Changed: height of stonework
22–23	24–25	Changed: length of bench
24	23–24	Added: person
26–29	07–09	Removed: cloud
26–29	15–19	Added: stone wall
27–30	02–04	Added: vulture
27	31–35	Removed: reed
28–29	20–21	Changed: height of stone
29–30	25–27	Added: plant
29–30	30–33	Added: table
29–30	20–23	Added: plant
29–30	34–35	Added: plant

PUZZLE 30

Central Park

Central Park is the most visited urban park in the United States. Located in the center of Manhattan, it opened in 1857 and today it offers a multitude of entertainment opportunities.

01	22	Added: red chair
01–03	04–06	Added: moon
01–03	12–15	Added: building
02	25–27	Changed: flipped person
02–03	20–22	Added: mounted police
02–04	16–21	Removed: tree trunk
03–06	33–34	Changed: bag, red to blue
03–07	25–27	Added: dog
04	12	Added: window
04–05	13	Added: window
05–06	19–23	Added: statue
06–07	11–12	Changed: striped pillar
07	23–24	Changed: scarf, yellow to purple
07	09–10	Changed: window
07–09	07–09	Added: height to building
08–09	22–23	Changed: flipped person
10	22	Removed: black bag
11	09–14	Removed: windows
11	25	Removed: soccer ball
11	26	Added: book
11–12	26–27	Removed: black cloth
12	08	Added: water tower
12	23–24	Added: black shirt
12–14	08	Changed: rooftop, white to red
12–18	21–22	Removed: black fence

15	14–15	Removed: building
15–16	32–33	Removed: shoe
17–19	11	Added: building construction
18–19	16–21	Added: floodlight
19–20	24–25	Changed: flipped seated person
19–21	30–31	Added: puddle
19–22	27–28	Removed: towel
21	12–13	Added: height to building
21	26–27	Added: extra leg
22	11–12	Added: flag
22	13	Added: clock
22–30	03–05	Added: jet trail
23	21–23	Added: person
23	15	Changed: banner, blue to red
24	10	Removed: window
24–25	20–21	Changed: building, brown to blue
25	09–10	Added: extension to building
27	11	Removed: water tower
27	12–17	Changed: banner, beige to blue
27–28	21–22	Added: umbrella
27–28	26–30	Added: fire hydrant
28–29	16–17	Changed: façade of window
28–30	19–21	Added: tree
29–30	13–14	Added: crane
29–30	22–25	Added: man

PUZZLE 31

Krakow

One of the oldest cities in Poland, Krakow dates back to the seventh century. This photograph shows the Cloth Hall in the city's Main Market Square. Known as the *Sukiennice* in Polish, it was once a major center of international trade, and today is home to a market, gallery, and museum.

01	13	Removed: doorway
01	14	Removed: tent
02–03	32–33	Removed: man (and his shadow)
02–04	06–07	Changed: height of roof
03–04	17	Added: square stall
03–05	27–28	Changed: plain bricks to red tiles
04–06	9–11	Added: picture of gorilla on screen
04–12	14–16	Added: second layer to railing
06–08	08	Added: skylight
07–08	28–30	Changed: umbrella, yellow to green
09	33–34	Added: people
10	17–18	Added: magazine stand
10–11	06–07	Changed: clock, black to white
11	20–22	Removed: lamppost
11–12	12–15	Removed: corner of building
12	08	Added: window
12	12	Changed: orb, yellow to pink
12	13	Removed: window
12	29–30	Removed: person (and shadow)
12–13	26–27	Removed: green table
12–13	31–32	Removed: umbrella
13	18–19	Removed: person
14	15	Added: section to window
15–16	08–10	Changed: building, blue to red
15	17–18	Removed: pillar

16	14–15	Added: window
16–17	21–22	Changed: color of table, green to purple
16–17	35	Added: person
17–18	07	Removed: decorative element on roof
17–18	19	Removed: magazine stand
17–19	22–23	Changed: red tiles to plain bricks
18–19	07–08	Removed: skylight in roof
18–19	20–23	Removed: tree
19	12–13	Added: flag
19	15–16	Added: skylight
22–23	08–09	Changed: roof, green to red
23	17	Changed: umbrella, orange to blue
23	21	Removed: walking man
23–26	25–28	Added: glass pyramid
24–25	08	Changed: roof, brown to green
25–27	23–25	Added: group of umbrellas
26	19–20	Removed: doorway
27	06–07	Added: extension to building
27	10	Changed: window
27–28	15–16	Changed: color of awning
27–28	17–20	Added: lamppost
27–28	21–22	Added: bookstall
29	08	Added: box on roof
29–30	12	Changed: awning, orange to blue
30	13–14	Added: leaves to tree

PUZZLE 32

Cinque Terre

Cinque Terre, meaning "The Five Lands," is a UNESCO World Heritage Site comprised of five villages situated off the beautiful Ligurian coast, northern Italy. Made up of Corniglia, Manarola, Monterosso al Mare, Riomaggiore, and Vernazza, Cinque Terre has become a popular off-the-beaten-path haven for adventurous tourists.

01	17–20	Added: train	17–18	23–24	Added: dinghy
01	21–26	Added: brick edging	17–19	05	Added: jetty
02	17–18	Removed: window	18	11	Added: window
02–05	03–04	Added: purple flowers	18–19	08	Removed: skylight
03–06	16–17	Changed: roof, red to green	18–19	18–19	Removed: rock
04	13	Added: window	20	05	Changed: house, orange to blue
05–06	03	Added: window	20	17–18	Removed: boulder
05–06	11–12	Removed: window	22–23	13	Added: steps
06	10	Removed: structure on roof	22–26	03–04	Added: whirlpool
06–07	07–08	Added: extension to awning	22–27	15–17	Added: seagull
06–09	16–17	Added: railings	24	10–11	Added: white sheet
10–11	22–24	Removed: boulder	24	14	Added: boat
10	17	Added: window	24–25	10–11	Added: sign
11–12	05	Changed: building, red to blue	24–25	19	Removed: boat
12–13	11	Removed: bell tower	24–30	01–02	Added: island
13–14	04	Added: extra story to building	25–26	21	Changed: boat, yellow and blue to blue and orange
13–14	15–17	Removed: doorway			
14	18–19	Removed: doorway	26	09–12	Changed: building, yellow to red
14–15	06	Changed: roof, red to yellow–brown	26–27	13–14	Added: boat
15–16	24–27	Removed: palm fronds	26–27	24	Removed: boat
15–17	02–03	Added: ship	27	08	Added: window
15–17	12–13	Added: extension to roof	27–29	04–05	Added: building
16	15–16	Added: window	28–29	09–10	Added: dormer window
16	17–18	Removed: archway	28–29	13	Added: awning
16–17	11	Added: window	29–30	21–22	Added: boat
			30	25	Added: buoy

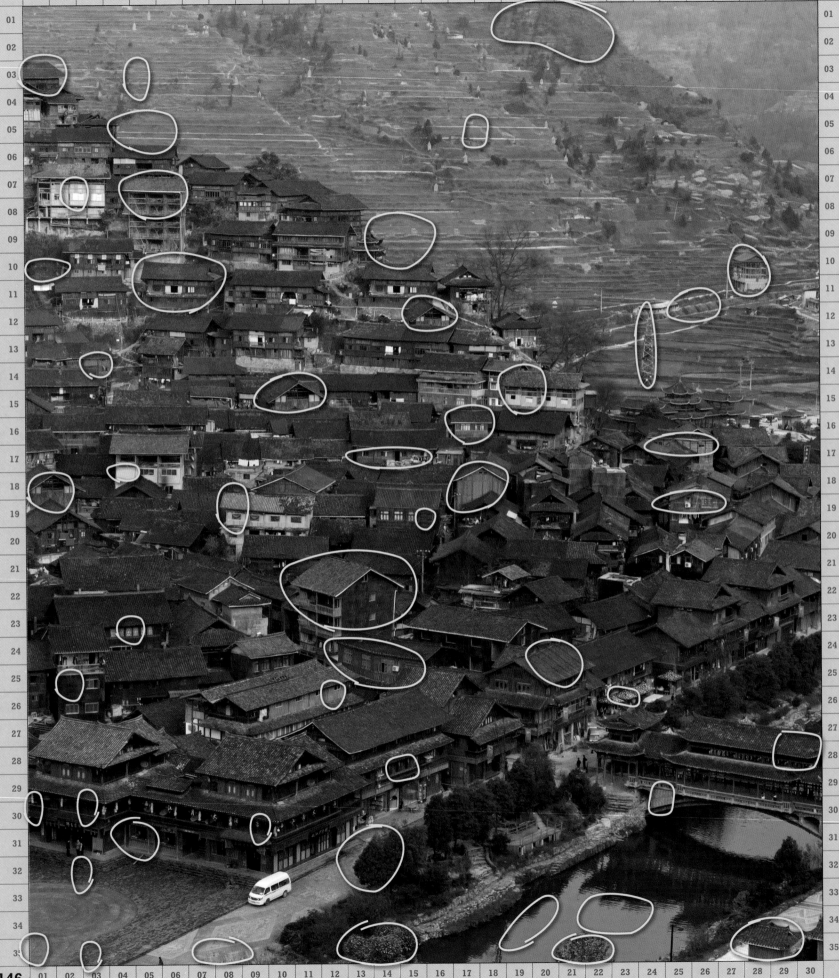

PUZZLE 33

Xijiang Miao

The village of Xijiang Miao, situated in the deep valleys of the Leigongshan National Park, eastern Guizhou, China, contains the world's largest population of the ancient Miao people. With over one thousand wooden houses built high into the steep hills, Xijiang is considered a "living fossil" of the Miao's history and traditional culture.

01	30	Removed: sign	12–15	34–35	Added: tree top
01	35	Removed: path	13–14	31–33	Added: tree
01–02	02–03	Added: building	13–16	08–10	Removed: building
01–02	10	Removed: green patch	13–17	20	Changed: building, brown to blue
01–02	18–19	Changed: building, brown to green	14–15	28–29	Removed: white sheet hanging from building
02	25	Removed: window	15–16	19	Removed: window
02–03	07–08	Changed: window covered	15–17	11–12	Added: building
02–03	32–33	Removed: person	16–18	15–16	Added: building
03–04	13–14	Changed: building, brown to green	17–18	05	Removed: tree
03	30	Removed: yellow flag	17–18	17–19	Changed: building, brown to blue
03	35	Removed: person	18–20	14–15	Added: extension to building
04	17–18	Removed: window	18–23	01–02	Changed: mountaintop raised
04–05	03–04	Removed: trees on hill	19–20	33–35	Removed: reflection
04–05	23	Added: windows	20–21	24–25	Removed: peaked roof
04–05	30–31	Added: building front	20–22	34–35	Added: tree top
04–06	05–06	Removed: building	22–24	33–34	Removed: reflection
04–07	07–08	Added: building extension	23	26	Added: blue and white square umbrella
05–07	10–11	Added: building	23–26	16–17	Changed: building, brown to green
07–09	35	Removed: tree top	24	12–14	Added: pylon
08	18–19	Added: building extension	24–25	29–30	Removed: arch
09	30–31	Removed: yellow flag	25–26	11–12	Removed: building
09–12	14–15	Added: building	25–27	18–19	Changed: building, brown to green
10–14	21–22	Added: extra story to building	27–28	10–11	Added: building
12	25–26	Added: panel to building	27–30	34–35	Added: building
12–15	24–25	Changed: building, brown to blue	29–30	27–28	Added: extension to pagoda

PUZZLE 34

St. Peter's Square

This vast plaza is located directly in front of St. Peter's Basilica in the Vatican City. At the center of the square is an Egyptian obelisk dating back to 2400 BC. It was transported to the site in 1586.

01	25–26	Added: sign
01–03	30–33	Removed: white line
01–35	01–03	Changed: clouds
02	28–29	Removed: statue
02–06	08–11	Added: church
03	34–35	Changed: window, yellow to blue
04–05	26–28	Added: fountain
05	21–22	Removed: statue
05–06	13–14	Added: building
05–06	17–18	Added: rooftop unit
06–07	31	Added: tent
07–08	32–35	Added: statue
08	22	Changed: window, green to purple
08	24	Added: tree
08–09	16–17	Added: chimney
10	07–08	Added: dome
10	27–31	Removed: chairs
11	15–16	Added: tree
11–13	22	Removed: crosswalk
12	20	Removed: window
13	09	Added: tower
13	11	Added: door
15	18–19	Changed: bus, yellow to red
15	22	Removed: vehicle
15	22–23	Removed: vehicle

15–17	09–13	Added: church
15–16	32–34	Changed: St. Andrew's cross, green to red
15–24	35	Changed: floor, brown to blue
16–17	19–21	Changed: height of obelisk
17–18	11	Added: boat
17–21	05–06	Removed: trees
18–19	19–20	Changed: window
18	24–30	Removed: ground marking
19–20	12	Removed: arch
20–22	26	Removed: fence
20–21	31–32	Added: traffic cone
21–22	15	Removed: chimney
22–23	12–13	Added: boat
22–24	27–28	Added: seats
23	16–18	Added: chimney
23–24	21–23	Added: banner
24–25	12	Changed: roof, gray to brown
24–25	19–20	Added: window
26–27	09–10	Changed: height of building
27	15	Removed: round window
28–29	07	Added: tower
28–29	28	Changed: water, green to blue
28–30	14–15	Changed: wall, orange to red
28–30	17	Added: crenellations
28–30	19–21	Changed: building, yellow to red

PUZZLE 35

Thanksgiving Day Parade

Macy's Thanksgiving Day Parade in New York City is one of the largest parades in the country, and has been televised nationally since 1952. The tradition of the three-hour event started in 1924 with everything from floats to live animals. Gigantic balloons replaced the live animals in 1927.

01–02	22–23	Removed: letters "DUA"	18–19	20–21	Added: brass instrument
02–03	02–04	Changed: height of window	19	01–02	Removed: window
02–03	23–25	Changed: sign, red to yellow	19–21	21–22	Changed: sign, red to green
04–06	21–23	Changed: height of shutters	20	01–02	Changed: height of window
04–05	29	Changed: coat, red to blue	21	02–03	Removed: window
05–06	06–08	Removed: window	21–22	05–06	Removed: sign
05–06	19–20	Removed: pharmacy sign	22–23	03–04	Removed: windows
05	31–33	Removed: police officer	22	11–12	Removed: finger
06–07	11–14	Removed: window reflections	22	16	Added: white road stripe
06–07	23	Changed: jacket, green to red	23	18	Removed: police officer
07	20–22	Added: entrance	23–24	32–34	Removed: person
07–08	32–35	Removed: person	23–26	34–35	Removed: road marking
08	28–29	Removed: manhole	24	04–05	Changed: awning, yellow to blue
09	21–22	Removed: police officer	24–25	01–03	Removed: graphic from inflatable
09–11	15–17	Removed: shop sign	25–29	01–02	Changed: inflatable, pink to blue
11–12	03–04	Added: stone pattern	25	05	Removed: eye from inflatable
11–13	18–19	Changed: kiosk, blue to green	26	15–16	Removed: person
12–14	09–10	Removed: ear	26–27	25–27	Removed: person
12–13	23–25	Removed: white line	26–27	29	Removed: manhole
14–17	12–13	Changed: lips, yellow to red	27	06–07	Added: pink tower
15–17	02–03	Removed: stone trim	27	13–14	Removed: person
15	24–25	Changed: costume, green to purple	27–28	13–14	Changed: costumes, pink to blue
15–16	32–33	Changed: pants, green to red	27–28	24–26	Changed: costume, red to blue
16–17	29	Changed: vehicle, red to purple	28–29	21–22	Removed: letter "Y"
16–17	32–34	Removed: letter "N"	30	01–02	Removed: buttons from inflatable

PUZZLE 36

Dragon Boat Race

Dragon Boat racing is deeply embedded in Chinese culture. Enjoyed at traditional festivals and competitions, fifty or more paddlers row in unison as they compete against other boat teams. The sport is a skillful show of group harmony and athletic ability.

01	12–14	Removed: mountain
02	19–20	Changed: jacket, blue to yellow
02–03	14–15	Changed: sign, blue to red
03–04	16–17	Added: boat
03–04	30–31	Added: green shirt
03–07	14	Changed: bridge, topiary removed
04	21–22	Changed: shirt, yellow to green
04–06	17	Added: tarpaulin
06	21–22	Removed: boy
06–07	14	Added: green bus
06–08	32–34	Changed: shirt, green to red
07	18	Removed: blue buffer
07–08	23–24	Changed: shirt, blue to pink
07–09	05–13	Added: extra wing to apartment block
07–09	17	Changed: front of boat, brown to green
09–14	17	Changed: bottom of boat, gray to blue
09	23–24	Changed: hat, red to purple
10	18	Changed: tire, blue to red
10	23–24	Changed: shirt, blue to pink
11	12–13	Removed: flag
11	25–26	Removed: oar
11–13	14–15	Changed: rigging, red to yellow
12–13	17	Removed: lifesaver
12–18	27	Added: fishing rod
13–14	05	Removed: structure on top of apartment block

14–15	14	Changed: flag, pink to blue
15–16	16	Changed: boat, blue to green
16	16–17	Removed: hanging bag
16–17	07–08	Added: height to apartment block
17	29–30	Removed: sign
17–18	26–28	Changed: shirt, pink to yellow
18–19	17–18	Added: sea monster
19	13–14	Added: flag
19–20	15–16	Changed: sign, red to green
19–20	27–29	Changed: shirt, yellow to green
20–21	07–08	Added: height to apartment block
20–21	27–29	Removed: flag
22–23	12	Removed: sign
22–24	15–16	Changed: boat, blue to brown
24–25	16–17	Added: boat
24–26	04–05	Added: height to apartment block
25–26	10–12	Added: building
26–27	31	Added: antenna to dragon's head
27–28	05	Removed: top of building
28–29	06–07	Removed: top of apartment block
28–29	17–19	Added: buoy
29	11–12	Changed: Chinese character flipped 180°
29	14–15	Added: banner
29–30	15–16	Changed: boat awning, blue to pink
29–30	16	Removed: banner

PUZZLE 37

Salamanca

Salamanca's designation as European Capital of Culture in 2002, as well as being declared a UNESCO World Heritage Site in 1998, highlights just how wonder-filled this beautiful city is. Located in northwestern Spain, Salamanca is home to the country's oldest university, founded in 1134.

01	13	Removed: tower
01	15	Added: window
01–05	35	Removed: arm of chair
02	15	Added: window
02–04	21–23	Changed: shirt, brown to blue
03–04	04–06	Added: hot air balloon
03–04	13	Removed: antenna
04	19	Removed: plaque
04–05	21–23	Changed: shirt, brown to green
04–07	26–27	Removed: chair
05	14	Changed: skylight in roof
05	15	Added: window shutters
05	16–17	Added: window shutters
05–06	27	Removed: part of tabletop
06–07	18–19	Added: window shutters
06–08	28–30	Changed: chair, blue to pink
09	11–12	Removed: statue
10–11	14–15	Added: window shutters
11–16	27	Removed: shadows
12–13	22	Removed: seated person
12–14	28–30	Added: seagull
13	22–23	Added: black cat
14	19–20	Added: column
14–15	09	Removed: statues
15–16	11	Removed: bell
15–18	25–26	Added: playful dog
16	05–07	Removed: top of antenna
16–19	32–33	Added: grid cover
17	21–22	Added: jacket, red to green
17–18	19	Changed: plaque, tan to bright blue
19–20	11–12	Removed: statue
19–20	22–23	Removed: bag
19–20	25–26	Removed: dog
20–24	23–24	Added: bench
22	22	Removed: boy
22–26	26–28	Added: table settings
24	12	Removed: top of antenna
25	13	Removed: pillar
25	16–17	Added: window
25	18–19	Removed: windows
26	16–17	Added: window shutters
26	18–19	Added: window
26–30	32–35	Changed: tablecloth, red to blue
27–28	22–23	Removed: seated person
27–30	05–10	Added: hot air balloon
28	13	Removed: chimney
28	15	Added: window shutters
28	28	Removed: section of chair
28–30	24–26	Added: cat
29	15	Added: window

PUZZLE 38

Himalayas

Key Gompa monastery is located in the Himalaya mountain range at an altitude of 13,668 feet (4,166 meters) above sea level. The monastery is home to more than 200 monks, and its walls are covered with ancient murals.

01	20–21	Removed: person
01–05	11–15	Removed: part of building
02	09–10	Added: yeti
02–03	19–20	Added: door
02–04	28–29	Removed: big rock
04–06	03–05	Added: face in the rock
04–06	09–10	Added: balcony railing
05	22–23	Added: height to pole
05	10	Removed: terrace support
06	15–16	Changed: window blinds, blue to red
06–08	12–13	Added: big rock
08	03–04	Added: extension to roof decoration
08	05	Removed: orange circle
09	20–21	Removed: shutter
09–10	05–06	Changed: decoration, orange to red
09–10	27–28	Added: llama
09–12	33–35	Removed: bush
10	06	Added: wall with decoration
12	04–05	Removed: roof decoration
12	11–12	Added: window
12	04	Removed: roof decoration
12	11–12	Added: window
13–14	19–21	Changed: window
13–15	11–12	Changed: surface, whitewashed wall to stone
13–15	29–30	Added: gate

14	07–08	Added: window
15	06	Removed: water tank
15–17	26–28	Removed: rock
15–19	17–19	Added: story to building
16	07	Removed: yellow stripe
17	08–09	Removed: antenna
19	06–07	Changed: color of fence
19–20	09–10	Changed: color of window frame
20–21	12–14	Removed: pole
20–22	25	Changed: wooden platform to stone wall
21	08–09	Added: satellite dish
22	07	Removed: balcony post
22	09–10	Added: door
22–23	13–14	Changed: stone wall, now painted
23	23	Added: window
23–24	17–18	Removed: window
23–28	25–28	Added: building
26–28	13–15	Changed: building, gray to pink
26–28	16–18	Added: wall
26–29	32–34	Added: shrub
27	16	Removed: doorway in wall
27	29	Removed: pillar
27–30	09–12	Added: landslide
28–29	14–17	Removed: pole
28–30	21–23	Removed: building

PUZZLE 39

Battle of the Oranges

Italy's largest organized food fight takes place every February in the northern town of Ivrea. Thousands of pedestrians divide into nine teams and exchange a barrage of citrus fruit with other townsfolk in carts. The tradition is believed to date back to the thirteenth century.

01	19	Added: face paint
01–02	30–32	Changed: clothing, red to green
01–03	03–06	Changed: screen, blue to yellow
01–03	25–27	Changed: pants, green to blue
02	14	Changed: shirt logo
02	09	Added: oranges
04–05	16–17	Added: blue hat
04–07	23–30	Removed: person
05	19–20	Added: red hat
05–06	12–13	Changed: scarf, green to red
06	03	Added: tomato
07–08	08	Changed: head
07–09	32–33	Changed: pants, red to green
08	17–18	Added: giant orange
08–10	19–23	Changed: cart, pink to green
08–10	09–11	Changed: coat, green to purple
09	16–17	Removed: armband
09–11	30	Added: pineapple
10–11	33–34	Added: hair
10–11	06–08	Added: person
10–14	32–35	Changed: position of arm
11–12	03–04	Changed: coat, blue to red
11–15	01–02	Changed: blue cloth to brick
12	28	Added: giant orange
14	09	Added: half a mango

14–15	12–13	Added: logo
14–15	21–22	Added: monkey
15	05–06	Changed: pants, red to green
15–17	23–24	Changed: feather, green to pink
16	17–19	Removed: hanging tool
17–18	06–08	Changed: flipped person
17–18	09–10	Removed: arm
19–20	07	Added: mohawk
19–30	25–35	Added: horse
20	06–07	Removed: jacket logo
20–21	03–06	Removed: person
20–21	12–14	Removed: red shirt
21–22	03	Added: box
21–23	18–19	Added: arm
22–23	14	Added: banana
24–25	02–05	Added: person
25	23	Added: lime
25	17–18	Added: bag
25–27	11–14	Changed: coat, blue to red
26–27	23	Added: apple
26–28	19–20	Added: flipper
27–28	16–17	Removed: bag
28–29	06–07	Added: dreadlocks
29	01–04	Removed: person
29–30	16	Changed: jacket logo, spade to club

PUZZLE 40

Niagara Falls

Located on the border of Ontario, Canada, and New York, Niagara Falls is made up of three waterfalls: the American Falls, the Bridal Veil, and the Horseshoe Falls. It has a vertical drop of over 165 feet (50 meters). It produces the highest flow rate of any waterfall on earth, and the survival rate for daredevils jumping over the falls is 75 percent.

01	18	Added: shadow to cliff
01–02	11–12	Added: sailing ship
01–02	27–28	Removed: white surf on water
01–06	12	Removed: bridge
02	34–35	Removed: car
03–04	33	Added: car
04	12	Added: building
04–05	16	Removed: white tent
04–05	29	Changed: container extended
04–07	06–07	Added: Canadian goose in flight
05	28	Removed: car
05–07	34–35	Changed: structure, gray to green
05–08	17	Removed: green grass
06–07	17	Added: triangle of grass
06–07	19–20	Removed: rocks
07	32	Removed: car
07–08	31	Removed: planted bed
07–10	23	Removed: white surf on water
08	20	Removed: rocks
08	35	Removed: car
09–10	21	Added: rocks
09–10	34	Removed: car
09–11	15–16	Added: dry land
10	18–20	Added: waterfall
10–16	29–30	Changed: stripes on awning, yellow to blue

11–12	28–29	Removed: path
11–13	17	Removed: island
12–13	34–35	Removed: van
13	21	Removed: rock
13–14	28	Changed: grass extended
13–14	32	Removed: windows in roof
14–15	22	Added: boat, *Maid of the Mist*
14–15	26–27	Removed: road crossing
16–18	35	Changed: roof, now smaller
17–18	31	Removed: car
18–19	32–33	Added: building extension
20–21	26–28	Added: building
22–23	24	Removed: rocky edge
24–29	03–07	Added: Canadian goose in flight
25–28	16–17	Removed: waterline
25–28	26–27	Added: Canadian goose in flight
25–28	34–35	Added: green grass
27–28	21–22	Added: waterfall
27–30	20	Removed: white surf on water
27	30	Changed: grass extended across path
28	22–23	Removed: section of grass
28–29	27–28	Changed: path widened and grass reduced
28–29	32–32	Removed: curved path
28–30	18–19	Added: dry land
30	32	Removed: path

Photo Credits

The publishers would like to thank the following sources for their kind permission to reproduce the photos in this book.

page 16 Shutterstock/saiko3p, page 20 Getty Images/Vanderlei Almeida/AFP, page 24 Getty Images/The Image Bank, page 28 Getty Images/Lonely Planet Images, page 32 Getty Images/Lonely Planet Images, page 36 Shutterstock/Anastasios71, page 40 Shutterstock/Christian Wilkinson, page 44 Shutterstock/Ashwin, page 48 Shutterstock/Jess Kraft, page 52 Shutterstock/Viacheslav Lopatin, page 56 Getty Images/Moment, page 60 Shutterstock/dp Photography, page 64 Shutterstock/Kiev.Victor, page 68 Shutterstock/Kiev.Victor, page 72 Shutterstock/Sophie James, page 76 Shutterstock/Reidl, page 80 Shutterstock/leoks, page 84 Getty Images/Kelly Fajack/Photolibrary, page 88 Getty Images/Hoberman Collection/UIG, page 92 Shutterstock/Borya Galperin, page 96 Getty Images/Moment, page 100 Getty Images/Keith Levit/Design Pics, page 104 Shutterstock/DuongMinhTien, page 108 Getty Images/E+, page 112 Getty Images/Lonely Planet Images, page 116 Shutterstock/Adrian Reynolds, page 120 Shutterstock/Anton Ivanov, page 124 Shutterstock/Pablo Hidalgo, page 128 Getty Images/Menahem Kahana/AFP, page 132 Getty Images/Sylvain Sonnet/Photolibrary, page 136 Shutterstock/De Visu, page 140 Getty Images/Moment, page 144 Corbis/Keren Su, page 148 Shutterstock/Ivan Marc, page, page 152 Getty Images/Moment, page 156 Getty Images/TAO Images, page 160 Shutterstock/Botond Horvath, page 164 Shutterstock/Smit, page 168 Shutterstock/Paolo Bona, page 172 Shutterstock/Deymos Photo

Publishing Credits

Editorial Manager: Roland Hall
Editorial: Malcolm Croft
Puzzle checking: Richard Cater, Caroline Curtis, Richard Wolfrik Galland

Puzzle Creators: Danny Baldwin, Ryan Forshaw, Georgios Mardas

Designer: Tasha Lockyer
Creative Director: Clare Baggaley

Picture Research: Steve Behan

For Baker & Taylor:
Traci Douglas and Lori Asbury